Cosmic Cafe

Written by Janine Scott

Illustrated by Hannah Wood

The Cosmic Cafe,
In the wide Milky Way,
Was the first dairy diner in space.

It had comet-shaped chairs,
Bright stars on the stairs
And satellites all round the place.

Mars Mozzarella,
A cheese-loving feller,
Owned the Cosmic Cafe.

He grilled cheese for brunch.
He baked cheese for lunch,
And then helped to serve cheese all day.

The cafe's best waiter
Was a whizz with the grater.
He came from a planet named Brie.

Together they knew
Every cheese dish and stew,
And their cheese sauce was lovely to see.

Then, one afternoon,
The Man in the Moon
Came to the cafe to eat.

"The moon's made of cheese,
So I don't want that, please.
I'm looking for something quite sweet."

The waiter went red,
Steam shot from his head,
For cheese was his favourite food.

And Mars Mozzarella,
That cheese-loving feller,
Thought that the Moon Man was rude!

"I'll show him," he thought.
"I'll soon fix his sort."
And he rushed to the kitchen to cook.

He started to stir,
To dice, slice and whirr.
And his waiters all stopped by to look.

His sweet cake creation
Soon caused a sensation,
The loveliest thing he had baked.

It was smooth, round and white,
A cosmic delight,
Like a moon in the shape of a cake.

The Man in the Moon
Ate that cake with a spoon
Till nothing was left but white traces.

"This cake is a treasure!
I must have the pleasure
Of telling my friends in high places."

Soon Mars Mozzarella,
That cheese-loving feller,
Was famous, a Milky Way star.

They all knew his name,
And everyone came
By spaceship, spacebus and spacecar.

Now Mars Mozzarella,
That cheese-loving feller,
Has cafes all over the sky.

His favourite, they say,
Is the Cosmic Cafe,
But no one has ever guessed why.

Still, each afternoon,
The Man in the Moon
Comes in for his favourite treat.

The cafe's best waiter
Hides his cheese grater
And brings a moon cake to his seat.

But Mars Mozzarella
Has fooled that Moon feller.
His special moon cake is a fake.

And one day quite soon,
When there's a blue moon,
He'll tell him that treat is CHEESEcake!

The Moon Mouse
Written by Janine Scott
Illustrated by Hannah Wood

Just the size of a pocket
With a backpack rocket,
Mars Mouse hunts for cheese in deep space.

He zooms past stars
To cafes and bars,
And no one can keep up his pace.

The Man in the Moon
Had been watching since June
And guarding his home every night.

Its cheesy bright glow,
A yummy yellow,
Was ripe for a Mars Mouse's bite.

But hungry Mars Mouse
Still got to Moon House
And started to nibble and gnaw.

He ate the cheese stairs.
He ate the cheese chairs,
Then started to chew the front door.

The mouse nibbled and crunched
Till the ceiling was munched
And the walls were Swiss-cheesy with holes.

"This moon is so pleasant.
I'll make it a crescent,"
Said the mouse as he gnawed to his goal.

The Man in the Moon
Then started to swoon.
He knew that the mouse must be banished.

That hungry Mars Mouse
Had eaten his house,
And much of the moon had just vanished.

The Man in the Moon
Felt a terrible goon.
His moon was now only a sliver.

He left his cheese house
In search of the mouse.
No time to waste or to dither!

He soon found the robber
By following the slobber
And the smell of the stinkiest cheese.

For Mars Mouse now dribbled
As he gnawed and he nibbled,
And slept off his dinners at ease.

When Mars tried to fly
Way up in the sky,
He found he was frightfully fat.

He was simple to snatch,
A real easy catch.
But that wasn't the end of that.

The Man in the Moon
Gave Mars Mouse a spoon
And ordered some cheese to take out.

He made that Mars Mouse
Fix up his Moon House
By spreading the cheese all about.

Mars Mouse had soon
Made him a new moon,
Which takes us right up to the present.

Now Mars' monthly chore
Is to nibble and gnaw
The round moon right into a crescent.

But he never eats
Cheesy moon treats
When the moon should be full and round.

He has learned to say,
"No cheese today!
That's more than enough I've found!"

Now his name is Moon Mouse
With his own cheesy house
And moon cheese for lunch and for dinner.

And each month he fasts
While the full moon lasts,
But it's only the moon that gets thinner!

Ideas for Parents

- Reading with children is an important way of encoraging a love of books. It familiarises your child with the patterns of the written language and helps increase his or her vocabulary, assisting him or her on the road to literacy.
- Urge your child to join in with reading. Encourage him or her to finish sentences, try new words and read sections on his or her own. Always read the book a number of times. Repetition familiarises children with language patterns and makes it more likely that they will join in.
- Children learn best when an experience is enjoyable, so always make reading together a positive and fun experience.

Helping Children to Understand the Text and Build Reading Skills

The Cosmic Cafe

- Enjoy the illustrations and rhyming text. Encourage your child to find some of the rhyming words: *chairs/stairs*, *brunch/lunch*, and so on. Discuss the sounds that your child can hear. Are these rhyming sounds? Can your child think of another rhyming word, such as: *brunch/lunch/munch*?
- Ask questions as you read to make sure your child understands the story, such as: *Why didn't the Man in the Moon want cheese for lunch*?

The Moon Mouse

- Enjoy the rhyming text and the illustrations.
- Pay attention to repeated letters and phrases, such as *Mars Mouse*, and rhyming words, such as *night/bite*. Encourage your child to notice the letters that form the sounds, for example, *–ouse*: *house, mouse*.
- Ask questions to develop your child's understanding of the story, such as: *Why was Mars Mouse a problem for the Man in the Moon*? Discuss how the story ends.
- Talk about the way the moon changes in the sky and why this happens.

RACING TO SUCCESS!

Michelin tyres were first used in sport as long ago as 1891. Follow their success story in a great colour feature starting on page 69.

TIGER

ANNUAL 1986 ★ CONTENTS

 85037-616-5

£3·25

BILLY'S BOOTS
BILLY DANE OWNED AN ANCIENT PAIR OF FOOTBALL BOOTS THAT USED TO BELONG TO OLD-TIME SOCCER-STAR, "DEAD-SHOT" KEEN. IN SOME STRANGE WAY, THE BOOTS SEEMED TO ENABLE BILLY TO PLAY IN DEAD-SHOT'S STYLE. BILLY HAD BEEN CHOSEN TO PLAY IN THE WARNER CUP AGAINST CRAGGS SCHOOL... AND HE TRAINED HARD...
DEAD-SHOT KEEN USED TO TRAIN LIKE THIS WHEN HE WAS A BOY! HE RECKONED IT IMPROVED HIS DRIBBLING A LOT...
BILLY DANE
DEAD-SHOT HAD SOME IDEAS TO IMPROVE HIS SHOOTING, TOO! IT'S IN HIS BOOK, SOMEWHERE. I'D BETTER LOOK IT UP ...'COS MY SHOOTING IS HOPELESS!
AT HOME...
HERE IT IS! "DEAD-SHOT KEEN EXPLAINS HOW HE BECAME THE DEADLIEST SHOT IN FOOTBALL"...
"YOU MUST ALWAYS PICK YOUR TARGET"... SAYS KEEN. "IT'S NO USE BLASTING AWAY AND HOPING FOR THE BEST!"
KEEN HAD A SIMPLE METHOD OF TRAINING. HE TIED A DUST-BIN LID TO THE CROSS-BAR!

CHANGING THE POSITION OF THE DUST-BIN LID...
TOP CORNER! THAT'S THE MOST DIFFICULT SPOT FOR A GOALIE TO COVER!
PRACTISING FOR HOURS...
UNTIL HE COULD HIT HIS DUST-BIN LID TARGET NINE TIMES OUT OF TEN!
AT SCHOOL...
I'LL BORROW THIS. NO-ONE WILL KNOW...
KITCHEN STA ONLY
AND, AFTER LESSONS...
NOT AS EASY AS IT LOOKS! DOES HELP TO HAVE A TARGET, THOUGH!
GOT IT! THAT'S FOUR OUT OF SEVEN! I'M GETTING BETTER!
THEN...TROUBLE– THE HEADMASTER!
SO THAT'S WHERE THE DUST-BIN LID WENT! THE CANTEEN STAFF HAVE BEEN COMPLAINING ABOUT IT BEING MISSING. PUT IT BACK, DANE...AND STAY IN TOMORROW AFTER SCHOOL!
I CAN'T STAY IN TOMORROW, SIR. I'M PLAYING IN THE WARNER CUP!
YOU SHOULD HAVE THOUGHT OF THAT BEFORE! YOU'D BETTER TELL MISTER HARRIS YOU'LL BE WRITING LINES INSTEAD!

AND SO...
I-I THINK I'LL FINISH MY LINES BY THE TIME THE SECOND HALF STARTS, SIR.
WE'LL PUT SMITH IN THE TEAM, SIR... AND CHANGE BILLY TO SUB.
VERY WELL! DO THAT. IT'S THE BEST WAY OUT.
YOU'RE DAFT GETTING YOURSELF KEPT IN, BILLY. THE WARNER CUP IS ALWAYS A GOOD GAME!
I WAS ONLY PRACTISING! CRUMBS... HOPE I GET A CHANCE TO GO ON AS SUB... EVEN IF IT'S ONLY FOR THE LAST HALF HOUR.
AND...
IT'S THERE! RAAAY!
THEY'RE CHEERING. SOMEONE MUST HAVE SCORED! WISH I WAS OUT THERE...
LATER...
YESSS!
SOUNDS LIKE ANOTHER GOAL! HOPE IT'S US! MUST BE RIGHT ON HALF TIME, TOO!
IF YOU'VE FINISHED YOUR LINES, YOU MAY GO, DANE. AND DON'T REMOVE SCHOOL PROPERTY AGAIN, UNDERSTAND?
YES, SIR...
WHAT'S THE SCORE, SID?
ONE-ALL! GOOD GAME, TOO. ANYONE COULD WIN... THERE'S STILL HALF AN HOUR LEFT!
AH, DANE! I'M GLAD YOU'VE ARRIVED. YOU'LL HAVE TO GO ON. JIMMY DAWSON'S LIMPING BADLY. HE WAS OUR GOAL-SCORER, TOO!
POOR OLD JIMMY. STILL... GLAD I'M GETTING A GAME!

DANE'S COMING ON!
GOOD LUCK, BILLY...
THANKS...
HE CAN BE GOOD...
HE CAN BE TERRIBLE, TOO!
IT TOOK BILLY A WHILE TO GET INTO THE GAME...
HECK! HE'S REALLY FAST!
WAKE UP, DANE!
MARVIN SOAMES WAS IN THE GROUNDWOOD TEAM...
CHASE IT, MARV!
HE'S OFF-SIDE!
NO HE WASN'T. NOT WHEN THE BALL WAS KICKED! GOOD PASS FROM DANE.
OHHHHHHH! HARD LUCK, MARVIN!
CRACKING SHOT! SHAME IT WASN'T ON TARGET!
CRAGGS SCHOOL CAME BACK...
CRAGGS SCHOOL! CRAGGS SCHOOL!
BOBBY PEARSON'S GOING THROUGH ON HIS OWN! THIS COULD BE THE WINNER!
REG WOOD IN GOAL...
MAGIC, REG!
GREAT SAVE!

A MINUTE TO GO...
IT'S GOING TO BE A DRAW!
THAT'S A FAIR RESULT! IT'S BEEN A CRACKING GAME!
EACH TEAM WILL HOLD THE CUP FOR SIX MONTHS, I SUPPOSE!
BUT...
THE OLD BOOTS SEEM TO BE MAKING ME GO! SOMETHING'S GOING TO HAPPEN...
A LOVELY PASS FROM MARVIN. AND...
IT'S JUST LIKE DRIBBLING ROUND THOSE ROCKS WHEN I WAS OUT PRACTISING THE OTHER DAY...
SHOOT, DANE!
HIT IT! IT'LL BE YOUR LAST CHANCE. TIME'S UP!
AND THEN...
THE DUST-BIN LID!

YEESSSSS! BILLY DANE! MAGIC!
THAT WOULD HAVE HIT THE DUST-BIN LID... IF IT HAD BEEN THERE!
IT'S MY PLEASURE TO PRESENT THE WARNER CUP TO GROUNDWOOD SCHOOL!
THERE'S ONLY ELEVEN MEDALS, JIMMY! YOU GO UP!
THAT'S ROTTEN! YOU SCORED THE WINNER, TOO!
WHEN THE MEDALS HAD BEEN PRESENTED...
DANE! COME HERE! WE'VE GOT SOMETHING FOR YOU!
WE CAN'T LEAVE THE MATCH-WINNER OUT! SO HERE'S SOMETHING FOR YOU TO REMEMBER THE GAME BY!
OH! ER... THANKS, SIR...
A DUST-BIN LID! WHY IS DANE GETTING THAT?
'COS HE'S RUBBISH, I EXPECT! HAW, HAW!
BETTER THAN NOTHING! BIGGEST WINNER'S MEDAL I'LL EVER GET!
PRESENTED TO BILLY DANE
WARNER CUP
1986

OLYMPICS Extravaganza!

DESPITE political boycotts by most of the East European countries and Cuba, the 1984 Olympic Games were opened by President Reagan at the Coliseum, Los Angeles, in the most spectacular ceremony ever.

With aircraft above, and athletes on the ground, spelling out the word 'Welcome', thousands of helium-filled balloons were released, photo left, at the start of the opening ceremony. The Olympic Flame burns brightly at the top of the magnificent Los Angeles Coliseum, while spectators use special cards to make giant flags of all the competing countries, inset photo. Now turn the page for the action!

OLYMPICS Extravaganza!

'Golden boy' Seb Coe, below, became the first athlete to win the 1500 metres title in successive Olympics. Steve Cram, left of picture, took the silver for a great British 'one-two'!

The race of the Games was expected to be the 3000 metres duel between Zola Budd and Mary Decker, below. But a collision ruined both their chances of a medal.

... LOS ANGELES 1984 ... LOS ANGELES 1984 ... LO

Britain's 'big three' of Steve Ovett, Steve Cram and Seb Coe, above, in the 1500 metres final. But Ovett couldn't complete the race through illness. The faces of failure and success, left, with Mary Decker's anguish at falling in the 3000 metres and Seb Coe's patriotic joy of winning the 1500!

ANGELES 1984 ... LOS ANGELES 1984 ... LOS ANG

OLYMPICS Extravaganza!

America were top medal winners at L.A., with 83 golds, 61 silvers and 30 bronzes. Helping towards that huge haul, was 16 year-old Mary Lou Retton, pictured below on the asymmetric bars, who won the all-round gymnastics gold and individual silver and two bronzes.

... LOS ANGELES 1984 ... LOS ANGELES 1984 ... LO

On top of the pole vault — and his form — was Britain's Daley Thompson, who won the Decathlon with a new Olympic record of 8,797 points, to add a second gold to the one he won at Moscow in 1980. But the athletics King of the Games was America's incredible Carl Lewis, below left. Known as "the fastest human on earth", he won four golds — 100m, 200m, 4 × 100m relay and long jump — to equal Jesse Owens' 40-year-old Olympic achievement.

Dreams were fulfilled — and shattered, as a buckled wheel ends the cycle sprint hopes of Japan's Katsuo Nakatake, photo top of page. The 'Ghost Town' setting for one of the 3-day event sections, above, with Lucinda Green, a member of Britain's silver-medal winning team, in action.

ANGELES 1984 ... LOS ANGELES 1984 ... LOS AN

OLYMPICS Extravaganza!

In the same razzamatazz style that they had opened, the 1984 Olympics ended amid scenes worthy of a Hollywood film set! The spirit of goodwill was as bright as the fireworks — sport had triumphed over politics!

Autograph ALBERT
I'M AUTOGRAPH-HUNTING DOWN AT OUR LOCAL SPORTS CENTRE... I HOPE TO SEE SOME STARS!
I'M GOING TO PUT THE SHOT...
WHERE ARE YOU GOING TO PUT IT?
JUST WATCH MY STYLE...
EEEK! I MUST HAVE A HOLE IN MY POCKET. THOSE MARBLES HAVE FALLEN OUT...
HERE I GO...
ER... I THINK THERE'S SOMETHING YOU SHOULD KNOW...
SPIINNNNGGG!
OH, DEAR... HE'S IN A REAL SPIN!
ZIP!
YEOOOW!
ZOOM!
THAT'S GOING TO BE A WORLD RECORD!
THUD!
CRASH!
IT'S GONE STRAIGHT THROUGH THE ROOF OF THE GYM!
AND INSIDE...
JUST THIS SERVE TO WIN THE BADMINTON CHAMPIONSHIP...
BUT THEN...
AAARGH! MY FOOT!
SWISH!
CLUMP!
YEE-OOOW!
WHOOSH!
I'VE HEARD OF THE WINNER LEAPING THE NET IN TENNIS, BUT THIS IS RIDICULOUS!
WELL, I DIDN'T SEE ANY STARS... BUT I BET THEY DID!

INDIA V ENGLAND, 1st TEST

DECEMBER 1984

WANKHEDE STADIUM

Sivaramakrishnan — the unplayable leg-spinner with an unpronounceable name — was the star of India in their eight wicket win. He claimed twelve victims, including Tim Robinson, seen here

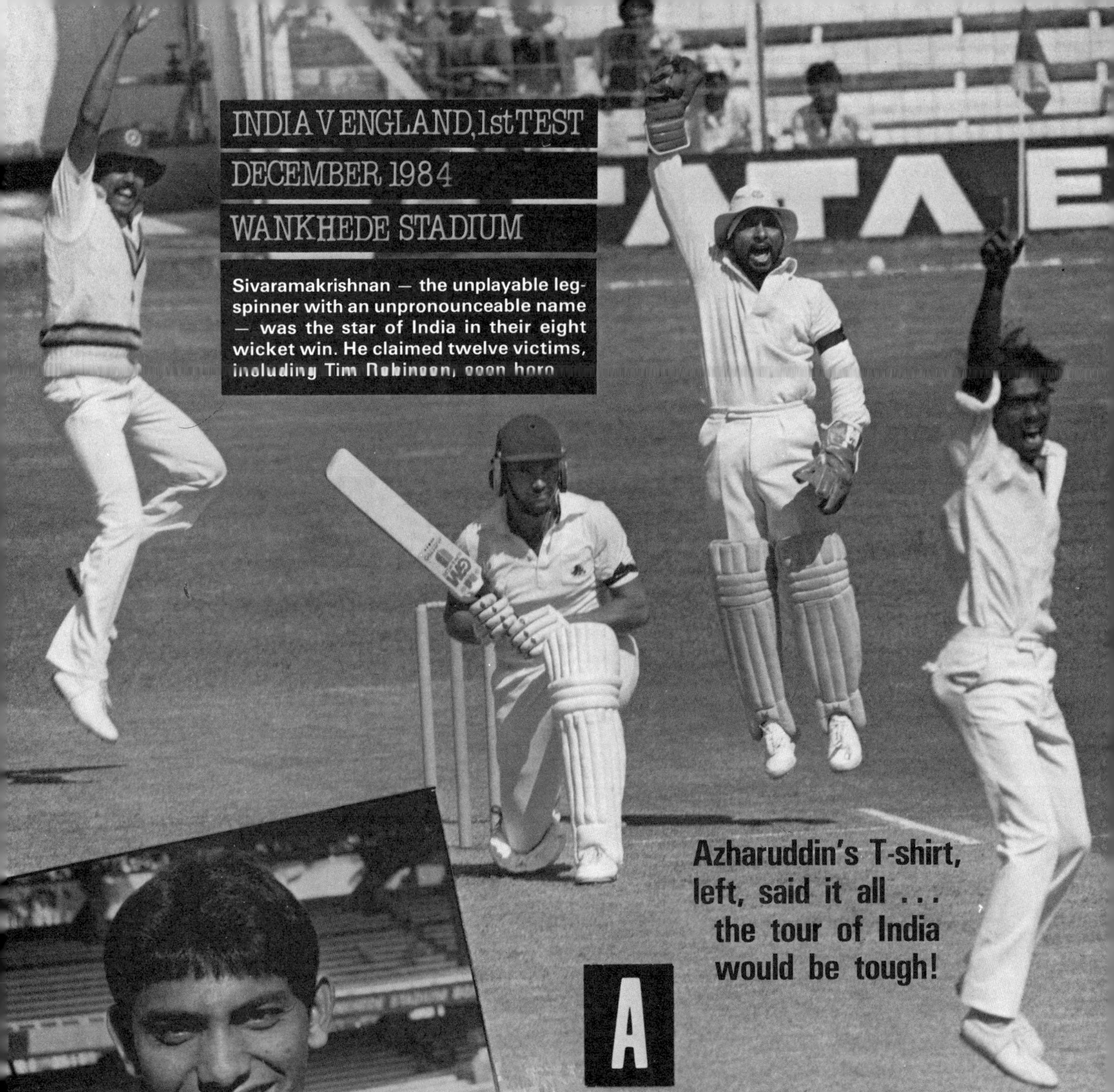

Azharuddin's T-shirt, left, said it all . . . the tour of India would be tough!

A TESTING TIME FOR ENGLAND!

2nd TEST
DECEMBER 1984
DELHI

In the First Test, Mike Gatting's battling batting offered hope for England. The cover drive pictured above brought up his first ever Test century. India's brilliant all-rounder Kapil Dev saw to it that England skipper David Gower was kept on his toes, right, in the Second Test, before Pat Pocock, below, stepped in to say, "Hello, hello, hello. What's all this then?" . . . and the game 'turned' England's way. Phil Edmonds and Pocock sent India spinning to defeat.

4th TEST

JANUARY 1985

MADRAS

It was like being at home for the English lads in the drawn Third Test . . . the game was held up by the rain! Essex paceman Neil Foster came into the side for the Fourth Test, and then tore through the Indian batting. Above, Indian skipper Sunil Gavaskar is clean bowled, to become one of Foster's eleven victims. Mike Gatting, below, sweeps the ball during his superb double century innings, while Graeme Fowler salutes his own double ton, top of next page. Doesn't that scoreboard look good to English eyes! It was the platform for a nine wicket win.

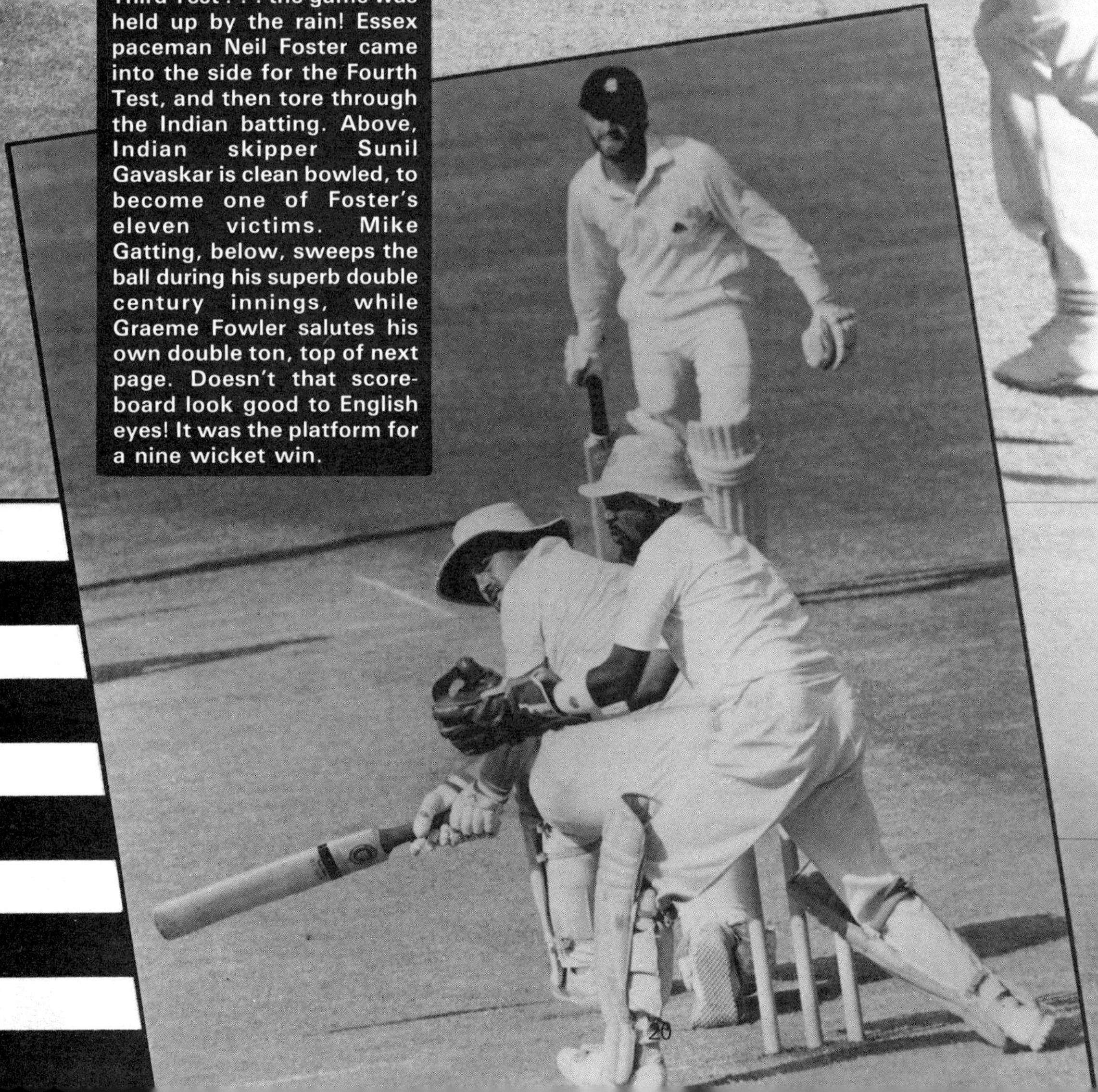

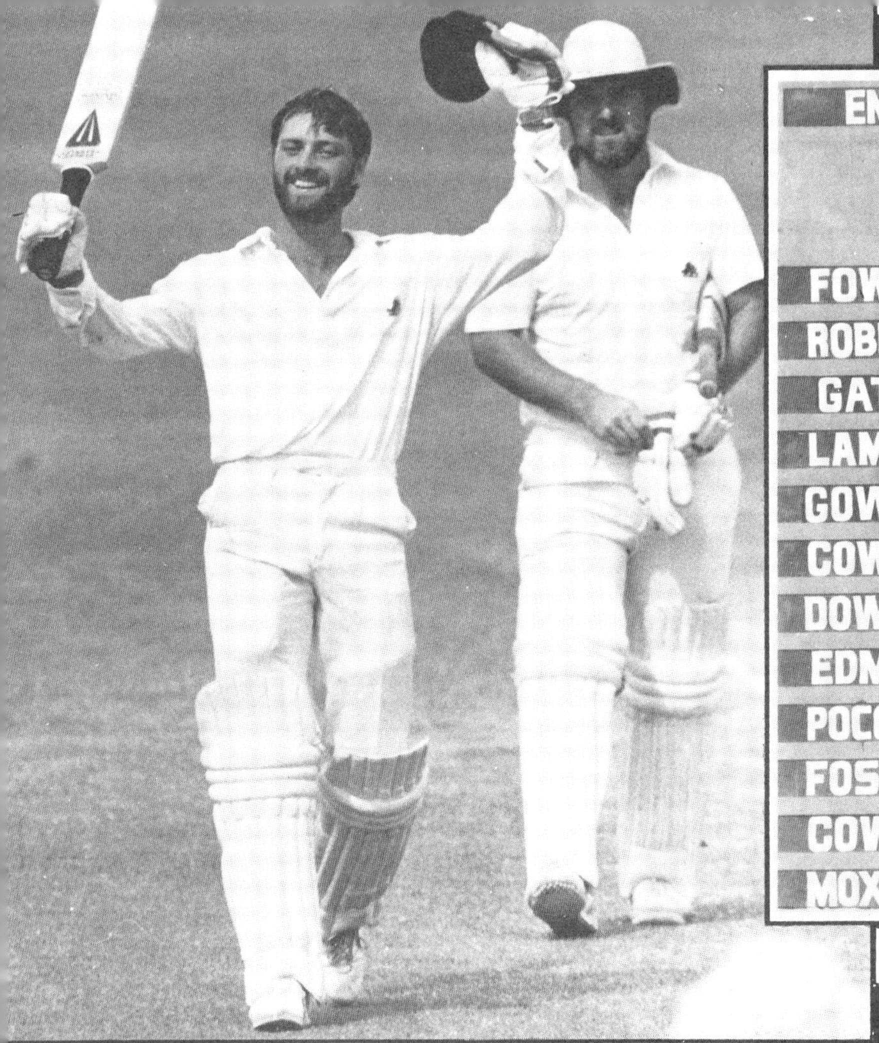

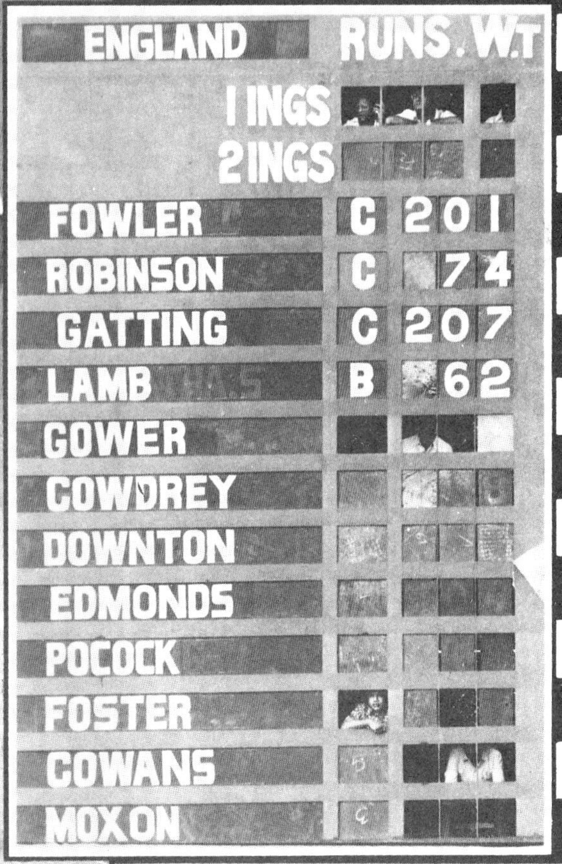

4th TEST JANUARY 1985 MADRAS

Fowler, Foster and Gatting, celebrate England's great victory. The Fifth Test was a draw, so England won the series!

DEATH WISH
BLAKE EDMONDS WORE A MASK, TO HIDE INJURIES TO HIS FACE. BLAKE WAS DEMONSTRATING HIS SKILL AS A PILOT...
JUST LOOK AT THAT!
IT'S WHAT YOU CALL SKILL!
BRILLIANT!
BLAKE EDMONDS CAN SURE PILOT A PLANE!
WHAT A GUY!
BLAKE FINISHED THE PERFORMANCE WITH A LOW-LEVEL PASS OVER THE GROUP OF ONLOOKERS...
ARRGH!
MY HAIRSTYLE!
BEAUTIFUL FLYING, OLD BOY... ABSOLUTELY SMASHING!
IT WAS WONDERFUL!
TERRIFIC!

YOU'RE ONE OF THE BEST PILOTS I'VE EVER SEEN.
THE VERY BEST!
GLAD YOU LIKED MY LITTLE SHOW, LADIES. IT WAS WARM WORK UP THERE!
THE GIRLS HAD LIKED HIS SHOW... BUT THEY DIDN'T LIKE HIS FACE!
EARGH!
UUH! WE... WE'VE GOT TO GO NOW.
T-TAKE US HOME, NIGEL.
WE DIDN'T REALISE HE WAS LIKE THAT!
TYPICAL! WHY ARE PEOPLE ALWAYS JUDGED BY APPEARANCES?
TAKE NO NOTICE OF THEM, BLAKE... THEY'RE NOT WORTH IT. I'VE REFUELLED YOUR 'COPTER. IT'S READY TO GO, WHENEVER YOU WANT.
THANKS, JAKE. I'LL HAVE A CUP OF TEA FIRST...
THAT PILOT WAS HORRIBLE. WHAT CAN WE DO TO FORGET HIM?
LET'S TAKE THE BOAT OUT. THE SEA'S A BIT ROUGH... BUT IT'LL BE EXCITING!

AND SO...
I'VE WARNED YOU...THERE'S A STORM COMING UP! IT'S NO DAY FOR MAKING PLEASURE TRIPS!
NONSENSE! THIS BOAT CAN STAND UP TO ANYTHING!
BUT JUST HALF AN HOUR LATER...
HECK! THE ENGINE'S CUT OUT!
STOP BEING SILLY, NIGEL... G-GET IT STARTED AGAIN!
I WANT TO GO BACK.
IT'S NO GOOD. IT'S PACKED UP COMPLETELY. WE...WE'LL HAVE TO SWIM FOR IT. THE BOAT'S TAKING TOO MUCH WATER TO STAY AFLOAT FOR LONG!
B-BUT I CAN'T SWIM!
NOR CAN I!
TOO BAD! IT'S EVERYONE FOR THEMSELVES! GOODBYE!
Y-YOU RAT... COME BACK!
THERE AREN'T ANY LIFEBELTS!
PLEASE, PLEASE... I DON'T W-WANT TO DIE!
SOON THE BOAT WAS WATERLOGGED...
WE...WE'RE GOING TO DROWN!
ARRRRRGH!
MEANWHILE, JUST A FEW MILES AWAY...
NO POINT IN WEARING A MASK UP HERE. THERE'S NO-ONE TO SEE ME!
MAYBE I SHOULD HAVE WAITED UNTIL THE STORM HAD CLEARED...

A FEW MINUTES LATER...
SOMEONE IN TROUBLE DOWN THERE... THEY LOOK IN A BAD WAY...
LUCKY THIS 'COPTER IS FITTED WITH A WINCH...
THAT'S IT, GIRLS... AND HURRY!
JUST IN TIME!
WELCOME ABOARD.
YOU YOU... SAVED OUR LIVES...
YOU... YOU'RE JUST WONDERFUL!
WONDERFUL!
AND LATER...
WE'RE GOING TO DINNER WITH A *REAL* MAN!
GIRLS! YOU'RE SAFE! THAT'S MARVELLOUS. I... *UUURGH!*
GET LOST, BUSTER!
SOMETIMES... JUST SOMETIMES... LOOKS AREN'T EVERYTHING!

WHo

A triple-hoop routine from British Champion, Steven Parks.

IF you thought that hula-hooping was simply trying to keep the hoop spinning round your waist, then think again! The makers of KP Hula Hoops — the crunchy potato snack — organised the British Hula Hoop Championships at 50 qualifying heats, with competitors having to show their expertise in blind moves, rapid switches and multi-hoops. Judges were the World male and female champions and they awarded the British title to Steven Parks (18) of Nottingham and the junior title to Joanne Morgan aged 10 of Newport.

World Champion Chico Johnson from California, poses with Steven Parks and Joanne Morgan.

oping It Up!

Female world title holder Melody Howe and Chico Johnson show the skill that spun them to world championship success!

Joanne was competing with 13-year olds, but still won the Junior title.

Chico shows Joanne how to keep up a whole heap of hoops . . . but he isn't holding that trophy!

FOOTBALL
"I'M WARNING YOU! YOU'RE NOT HELPING MATTERS BY CALLING ME 'BAGGY-PANTS'!"
"YOUR SOCKS REMIND ME OF OUR DEFENCE!"
"WOULD YOU BE QUIET! THERE'S A MAN HERE TAKING A PENALTY!"
"THE ONLY TIME WE STRUNG TWO PASSES TOGETHER, WAS WHEN WE KICKED OFF!"
MANAGER
"ER, BOSS, I KNOW I SAID I WANTED A BIGGER WAGE PACKET, BUT . . .
"ALL RIGHT! NO GAS – NO NICE HOT SHOWERS AFTER THE GAME!"
GASBOARD MEN AT WORK
"IT MAY SOUND SILLY . . . BUT I WANT YOU TO GIVE THEM EVERYTHING YOU'VE GOT AND DON'T GIVE ANYTHING AWAY !"
"BUT THERE WEREN'T ANY ARROWS ON THE FIELD,BOSS!"
TACTICS

"I SEE YOU'VE BEEN DISAGREEING WITH THE REFEREE AGAIN!"
"RIGHT THEN, YOU FORWARDS! ONE AT A TIME I WANT YOU TO DRIBBLE UP TO THIS LINE AND TRY TO SCORE!"
"I'M A BIT WORRIED ABOUT UNITED'S NEW TRAINER – HE THINKS TACTICS ARE A KIND OF SMALL MINT!"
ALL OF YOU
"DON'T WORRY ABOUT SATURDAY'S GAME – YOU'LL INJURE YOUR LEG IN TRAINING ON THURSDAY!"
MADAM ZARA TELLS YOUR FUTURE
"I WANT TO MAKE AN EARLY START FOR THE MATCH IN THE MORNING!"
FUNNIES
"MEET YOUR TEAM REPLACEMENT!"
"GREAT NEWS, BOSS! OUR GOALIE HAS CAUGHT SOMETHING AT LAST!"
"I WONDER IF THE BOSS IS ANGRY BECAUSE I MISSED THAT PENALTY?"

THE TOP MOTOR RACING DRIVER IN ONE OF HIS EARLY ADVENTURES!

SKID SOLO

In Mexico, motor racing star Skid Solo had agreed to drive in the Alvarez Invitation race—over 200 miles of dangerous mountain territory that once had been Inca land. Skid and his mechanic, Sandy McGrath, were staying with Senor Alvarez. Two days before the race, as Skid and Sandy inspected a section of the road...

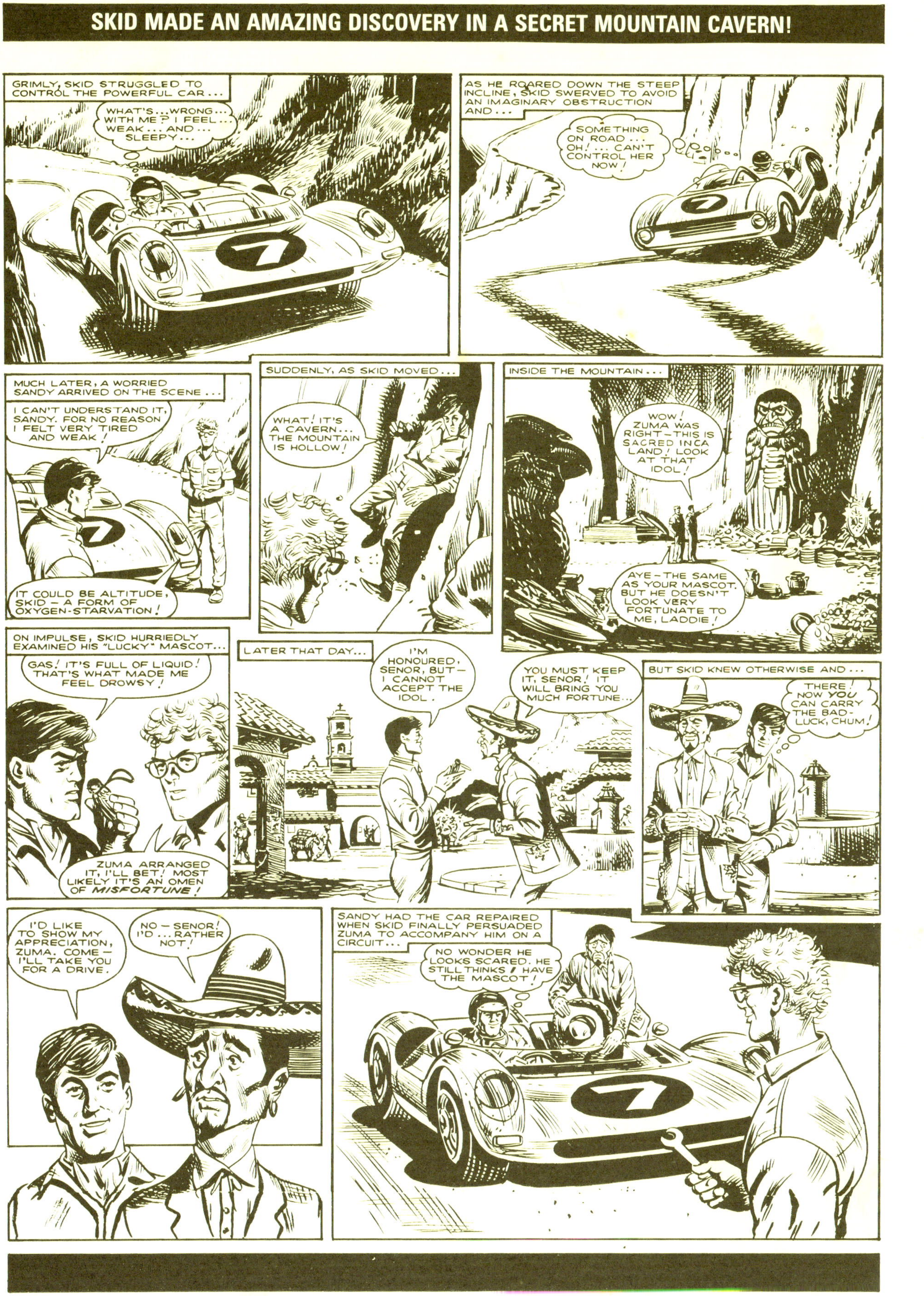
SKID MADE AN AMAZING DISCOVERY IN A SECRET MOUNTAIN CAVERN!
GRIMLY, SKID STRUGGLED TO CONTROL THE POWERFUL CAR ...
WHAT'S ... WRONG ... WITH ME? I FEEL ... WEAK ... AND ... SLEEPY ...
AS HE ROARED DOWN THE STEEP INCLINE, SKID SWERVED TO AVOID AN IMAGINARY OBSTRUCTION AND ...
SOMETHING ON ROAD ... OH! ... CAN'T CONTROL HER NOW!
MUCH LATER, A WORRIED SANDY ARRIVED ON THE SCENE ...
I CAN'T UNDERSTAND IT, SANDY. FOR NO REASON I FELT VERY TIRED AND WEAK!
IT COULD BE ALTITUDE, SKID - A FORM OF OXYGEN-STARVATION!
SUDDENLY, AS SKID MOVED ...
WHAT! IT'S A CAVERN ... THE MOUNTAIN IS HOLLOW!
INSIDE THE MOUNTAIN ...
WOW! ZUMA WAS RIGHT - THIS IS SACRED INCA LAND! LOOK AT THAT IDOL!
AYE - THE SAME AS YOUR MASCOT. BUT HE DOESN'T LOOK VERY FORTUNATE TO ME, LADDIE!
ON IMPULSE, SKID HURRIEDLY EXAMINED HIS "LUCKY" MASCOT ...
GAS! IT'S FULL OF LIQUID! THAT'S WHAT MADE ME FEEL DROWSY!
ZUMA ARRANGED IT, I'LL BET! MOST LIKELY IT'S AN OMEN OF MISFORTUNE!
LATER THAT DAY ...
I'M HONOURED, SENOR, BUT - I CANNOT ACCEPT THE IDOL.
YOU MUST KEEP IT, SENOR! IT WILL BRING YOU MUCH FORTUNE ...
BUT SKID KNEW OTHERWISE AND ...
THERE! NOW YOU CAN CARRY THE BAD-LUCK, CHUM!
I'D LIKE TO SHOW MY APPRECIATION, ZUMA. COME - I'LL TAKE YOU FOR A DRIVE.
NO - SENOR! I'D ... RATHER NOT!
SANDY HAD THE CAR REPAIRED WHEN SKID FINALLY PERSUADED ZUMA TO ACCOMPANY HIM ON A CIRCUIT ...
NO WONDER HE LOOKS SCARED. HE STILL THINKS I HAVE THE MASCOT!

THE INCA LEADER WAS MADE TO SEE THE ERROR OF HIS WAYS!

Hi, pals! How clued-up on sport are you? This quiz will really test your knowledge! Score two points for each correct answer, or part of an answer, then check your star rating at the foot of page 36.

1. I'm starting with cricket. Pictured on the left is the badge of a county side who won five one-day competition titles between 1978 and 1983. Name the club and the two West Indies Test stars who play for them.

answer GLAMORGAN Gavaskar

2. Two famous sports stars, who have both captained their country — but at different sports — are pictured above when they received honours at Buckingham Palace in February 1985. Name them and the clubs they were with at the time.

answer KD Liverpool

3. One of the most famous team trophies in tennis is seen on the right, held aloft by the 1984 winners. Among them is Mats Wilander. Name the trophy, the country that won it and the country they beat in the final.

AMERICA WGERMANY

answer

...SPORTS QUIZ...SPORTS QUIZ

...SPORTS QUIZ...SPORTS QUIZ

4. Pictured below, are four soccer stars who were all with the same club at the time the photo was taken. Can you name them and the club? They have all won international caps, involving three different countries! Can you name those countries? Finally, who is the club's manager?

answer ENGLAN[D] SCOTLAN[D] DENMAR[K]
STRACHAN
BRAZIL
ROBSON
OLSEN
ATKINSON

5. Although the snooker player pictured above, has never won the World individual championship, he's twice won the World Doubles title with Steve Davis. Name him.

TONY MEO

answer

6. Photo left, is one of Britain's top sprinters. He finished 5th in the 1984 Olympics 100 metres final, recording a personal best time. In 1982, he tied for the Commonwealth 100 metres title with Allan Wells. Who is he?

MIKE McFARLANE

answer

7. The soccer star seen beating his opponent in the photo on the right is better known for another sport. Who is he? For which non-league Somerset team was he making his debut in January 1985?

IAN BOTHAM
BATH

answer

...SPORTS QUIZ...SPORTS QUIZ

8. The ski-ing star seen left, has earned the title of the 'King of Slalom', with around 80 World Cup individual wins. He also won two gold medals at the 1980 Winter Olympics. Name him and his country.

answer

9. The soccer star pictured right, proudly displays the fantastic six centuries of League appearances that he reached in October 1984. Can you name him and the First Division side he was skippering at the time?

answer

10. Touring with the England cricket team takes the players to fascinating parts of the world. First, can you name the cricketer pictured with his wife, above? Name the country where the photo was taken and the building in the background. Who won the 1984-85 Test series there?

answer

1 S	H	O	O	2 T	I	N	G	■
C	■	■	■	O	■	■	■	3 I
4 R	O	D	■	T	■	■	■	C
A	■	■	■	5 T	H	R	E	E
B	■	■	■	E	■	■	■	R
6 B	A	T	O	N	■	■	■	I
L	■	■	■	H	■	7 F	A	N
E	■	■	■	A	■	■	■	C
■	8 O	L	Y	M	P	I	C	S

11. Now try the crossword, left. Clues, across: 1. Sport at which Malcolm Cooper won gold for Britain at the 1984 Olympics. 4. Used for fishing. 5. Value of green ball in snooker. 6. Relay racers carry it. 7. Sports supporter. 8. World's top sporting spectacle held every four years. Clues, down: 1. Word board game. 2. British soccer club who won the 1984 UEFA Cup competition. 3. On which Torvill and Dean competed.

12. Lastly, can you name the soccer club that the badge shown below belongs to? What is the name of their famous chairman? Which side did they lose to in the 1984 F.A. Cup Final?

answer

QUIZ ANSWERS

(1) Somerset. Viv Richards and Joel Garner. (2) Keith Fletcher (Essex C.C.C.) left, and Kenny Dalglish of Liverpool F.C. (3) The Davis Cup, won by Sweden, who beat America. (4) Left to right: Gordon Strachan (Scotland), Alan Brazil (Scotland), Bryan Robson (England). Jesper Olsen (Denmark). They were all with Manchester United, managed by Ron Atkinson. (5) Tony Meo. (6) Mike McFarlane. (7) Ian Botham, Yeovil Town. (8) Ingemar Stenmark, Sweden. (9) Steve Perryman, Tottenham Hotspur. (10). Phil Edmonds. India. The Taj Mahal. England won. (11) Across: 1. Shooting. 4. Rod. 5. Three. 6. Baton. 7. Fan. 8. Olympics. Down: 1. Scrabble. 2. Tottenham. 3. Ice Rinks. (12) Watford. Elton John. Everton.

STAR RATING

★★★★★ 66 – 86 POINTS

★★★ 44 – 64 POINTS

★ 22 – 42 POINTS

STAR RATING

Golden boy
JAMIE SPEED, THE WONDER BOY ATHLETE, HAD BECOME A HOUSEHOLD NAME SINCE HE HAD WON DOUBLE GOLD AT THE OLYMPIC GAMES IN LOS ANGELES. NOW HE WAS ON A CHARITY TOUR...
293
AND NOW FOR THE EVENT OF THE DAY... THE GOLDEN BOY AGAINST BLUE WHISKY, THREE TIMES WINNER OF THE GRAND NATIONAL HERE AT AINTREE...
THEY'RE OFF!
IT WAS BOY AGAINST RACEHORSE ROUND THE SPECIALLY MODIFIED COURSE...
THIS IS A GREAT IDEA... BUT IT'S TOO ONE-SIDED! JAMIE SPEED'S GOT NO CHANCE OF WINNING!
YOU'RE RIGHT. A HORSE WILL ALWAYS BEAT A HUMAN!
NEXT MOMENT...
YOU'RE WRONG! JAMIE SPEED WILL BEAT THE HORSE BY .004 OF A SECOND!
WHAT? HOW DO YOU KNOW THAT?

MY COMPUTER TOLD ME! FEED IN THE RIGHT DATA AND YOU ALWAYS GET THE RIGHT ANSWER!
MEANWHILE, JAMIE HAD TAKEN THE LEAD, WITH HIS BARE FEET FLYING EFFORTLESSLY OVER THE RACECOURSE...
...AND SOARING GRACEFULLY OVER THE JUMPS...
BUT...
BLUE WHISKY'S GAINING FAST!
RACING WEEKLY
I KNEW IT! COMPUTERS OR NOT, THERE'S NO WAY TWO LEGS CAN EVER BEAT FOUR!
A GOOD TRY BY THE GOLDEN BOY, THOUGH.
THE CROWD HAD RECKONED WITHOUT JAMIE'S FAMOUS FINISHING BURST, HOWEVER!
UUUHHH!
LOOK AT HIM GO! WHAT A SPRINT FINISH!
HE'S MAKING THE HORSE LOOK AS THOUGH IT'S GOING BACKWARDS!
JAMIE SPEED'S JUST DONE IT! BY A WHISKER!
BUT SO CLOSE! WHAT A RACE! WHAT A FINISH!

WELL... WHAT DID MY COMPUTER PREDICT?
FOUR HUNDREDTHS OF A SECOND! HE GOT IT RIGHT! SPOT-ON!
NICE RUN, JAMIE. YOU TOOK THEM ALL BY SURPRISE THEN... ESPECIALLY BLUE WHISKY AND HIS JOCKEY!
IT WAS GOOD FUN, SERGEANT JOE... AND IT ALSO MADE A LOT OF MONEY FOR CHARITY!
POLICE SERGEANT JOE NORMAN WAS JAMIE'S COACH.
AND THEN...
EXCUSE ME, MY NAME'S KEVIN. YOU RAN A GOOD RACE, JAMIE... BUT YOU COULD HAVE EXTENDED YOUR LEAD TO A 1.03 SECOND MARGIN IF ONLY YOU'D TAKEN THE JUMPS MORE CLOSELY!
HUHH! WHAT THE–?
HANG ON, SERGEANT JOE...
HOW DO YOU KNOW THAT, KEVIN?
SIMPLE. MY COMPUTER SAYS SO. IF YOU FEED IT ACCURATE INFORMATION, IT CANNOT LIE!
ALL RIGHT, YOUNG KEVIN... WE'LL PUT YOU AND YOUR MAGIC COMPUTER TO THE TEST.
I'VE GOT THREE OTHER ANIMAL RACES THIS WEEK. LET'S SEE HOW CORRECTLY YOU ASSESS THEM!
JAMIE v. GREYHOUND...
JAMIE WINS... BY 0.9 OF A SECOND!
0:90

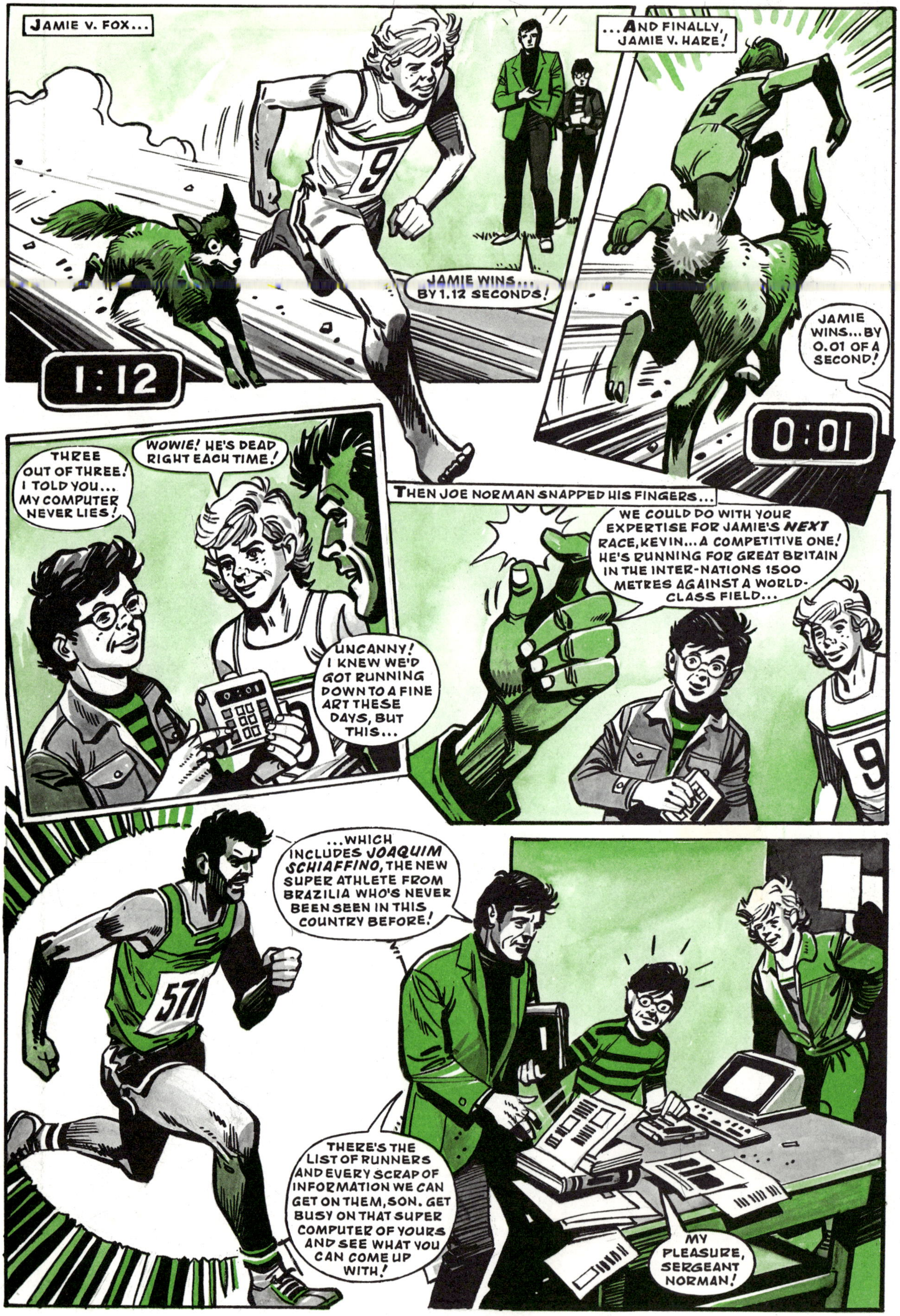
JAMIE V. FOX...
JAMIE WINS... BY 1.12 SECONDS!
1:12
...AND FINALLY, JAMIE V. HARE!
JAMIE WINS... BY 0.01 OF A SECOND!
0:01
THREE OUT OF THREE! I TOLD YOU... MY COMPUTER NEVER LIES!
WOWIE! HE'S DEAD RIGHT EACH TIME!
UNCANNY! I KNEW WE'D GOT RUNNING DOWN TO A FINE ART THESE DAYS, BUT THIS...
THEN JOE NORMAN SNAPPED HIS FINGERS...
WE COULD DO WITH YOUR EXPERTISE FOR JAMIE'S NEXT RACE, KEVIN... A COMPETITIVE ONE! HE'S RUNNING FOR GREAT BRITAIN IN THE INTER-NATIONS 1500 METRES AGAINST A WORLD-CLASS FIELD...
...WHICH INCLUDES JOAQUIM SCHIAFFINO, THE NEW SUPER ATHLETE FROM BRAZILIA WHO'S NEVER BEEN SEEN IN THIS COUNTRY BEFORE!
THERE'S THE LIST OF RUNNERS AND EVERY SCRAP OF INFORMATION WE CAN GET ON THEM, SON. GET BUSY ON THAT SUPER COMPUTER OF YOURS AND SEE WHAT YOU CAN COME UP WITH!
MY PLEASURE, SERGEANT NORMAN!

BEST TIME OF 3.32.4... LAST LAP OF 52.2... BUT RUNS WIDE ROUND FIRST BEND...
TWO DAYS LATER...
IF YOU WANT TO BEAT JOAQUIM SCHIAFFINO, JAMIE... YOU WILL HAVE TO WIN IN 3.23.2 SECONDS!
WHAAAT? BUT THAT'S ABOUT SEVEN SECONDS INSIDE STEVE OVETT'S WORLD RECORD! I CAN'T DO THAT!
IMPOSSIBLE!
SORRY– THE COMPUTER NEVER LIES!
AND SO TO THE DAY OF THE HIGHLY PRESTIGIOUS INTER-NATIONS 1500 METRES...
TO YOUR MARKS. SET...
LOOK AT THAT! JAMIE'S DASHED STRAIGHT INTO THE LEAD!
BUT HE'S RUNNING SO FAST, HE COULD BE DOING THE HUNDRED METRES SPRINT!
JOAQUIM SCHIAFFINO'S GONE WITH HIM!
THEY'RE WELL CLEAR OF THE FIELD ALREADY! BUT THEY'LL NEVER LAST AT THIS PACE... IT'S DAFT!
UUHHH! IT'S... HURTING. BUT I'VE GOT TO DO IT. IT'S THE ONLY WAY...!

TWO LAPS GONE... AND JAMIE'S LEAVING THE BRAZILIAN NOW. HE'S DESTROYED THE FIELD!
SCHIAFFINO'S DROPPED OUT! JAMIE'S RUN HIM INTO THE GROUND AFTER THAT LIGHTNING START!
IT THREW HIM OUT OF HIS PACE COMPLETELY!
JAMIE EASED OFF...
JAMIE SPEED WINS FOR GREAT BRITAIN!
IN A GOOD TIME, TOO... BUT IT WASN'T IMPORTANT. HE BEAT SCHIAFFINO, THAT'S WHAT MATTERED!
I-I WAS WRONG! BUT WHAT... HAPPENED? MY COMPUTER DIDN'T PREDICT THE CORRECT TIME...
YOU FORGOT ONE IMPORTANT THING, KEVIN...
COMPUTERS ARE VERY IMPORTANT THESE DAYS, BUT YOU SHOULD NEVER OVER-LOOK HUMAN BEINGS...
...THEY'RE UNPREDICTABLE... SOMETIMES THEY DON'T PERFORM LIKE MACHINES!

WHAT'S GOING ON?

Soccer can be a cut-throat game, as England star Peter Withe found out when Jimmy Greaves shaved him for charity!

HERE'S the pick of some of the more unusual pictures from our files!

An arresting appeal for LBW by the Brixton Police team 'keeper, right! But it wasn't a 'fair cop', because Brixton West Indies cricket club batsman Howard Chambers was given "not out"!

Something tells us that the mast of the boat, right, wouldn't go under Tower Bridge. It didn't . . . and the bridge was raised to allow Chay Blyth and Beefeater II to start an attempt to beat a 132-year-old sailing record. But the record still stands because Beefeater sank!

Photo left: part of an advertising hoarding at Headingley cricket ground isn't very complimentary to the fans in the seats behind!

Is this a water hazard, above? Yes, Spurs' striker Mike Hazard was hoping his side would make a splash in the 1984 UEFA Cup Final — and they did! 'Water' win!

"The fight's a fix!" yelled the crowd. And they were right, because top British heavyweight boxer Frank Bruno didn't 'stand' a chance against his 8-year-old opponent, after Jimmy Savile had 'fixed it' for would-be champ Ryan Stobie of Fife, as part of Jim's new 1985 TV series!

What's happened here, below? Did the batsmen just vanish into thin air . . . or did the bowling attack cause them to make a run for it? Neither . . . a Test between England and New Zealand was hot work, so it was helmets and gloves off for a cool-drink break!

WHAT'S GOING ON?

England and Man. United star Bryan Robson gets the boot — after scoring against Arsenal, too! Actually, Bryan had given the shot all he'd got — including his boot! So the Gunners were firing it back!

Meet fighting fireman Terry Marsh, left of pic, who put out the fire of former British Light Welterweight champ Clinton McKenzie with a scorching win!

The amazing running shoe pictured right, has a built-in computer that will 'jog' your memory on distance covered, speed, and even consumption of calories! There's only one thing it WON'T do for you . . . and that's to win the race on its own!

If you don't want to bite your nails, then get someone else to do it for you! At least that's how it seems in this photo of Chelsea's Keith Jones challenging Saints' Alan Curtis!

What's going on here? Have they found the Loch Ness monster at last? No, it was an aluminium model of a Tyrannosaurus Rex dinosaur being transported to a zoo in Sweden, where it will be used as a 'monster' children's slide!

There's nothing like relaxing by a pool with a cup big enough to take a long, cool drink, as Liverpool boss Joe Fagan demonstrates after his team had won the European Cup!

When George Meegan of Rainham, Kent, went out for a walk . . . he returned seven years later having covered 19,019 miles! Photo above: George proudly displays his Guinness Book of Records certificates for the longest walk in history, from the tip of South America to the wilderness of Northern Alaska. What a 'feet'!

Is Coventry City goalkeeper Steve Ogrizovic, right, trying to play snooker or table football? We're not quite sure, but it was a 'cue' for an amusing photo!

Loretta Doyle and Karen Briggs, below, believe in getting to grips with things . . . which is hardly surprising as they are members of the British Women's Judo Team! As well as holding each other, they have both held world titles in their respective weights!

Recognise the soccer star who was hoping to 'brew up' trouble for England? It's Scotland striker Kenny Dalglish, pictured visiting a soft drinks factory before the 1984 Scotland v England game. There's nothing soft about the Scots, but Kenny's potion only partly worked, because the match ended in a draw!

WHAT'S GOING ON?

WATER SKI-ING IS ANYTHING BUT PLAIN SAILING!

Going... ...Going ...Gone!

GREAT BRITAIN water-skier Martin Collins is really keen on his sport — in fact he was head-over-heels about it! Top photographer Chris Cole was on the spot at an international competition at Thorpe Park, to snap these photos of Martin's jump that went wrong. Fortunately, Martin was unhurt — but he couldn't even blame the boat driver, because there wasn't one! He was being towed by an automatic cable!

THE BARBED-WIRE X1
A GROUP OF WORLD WAR TWO EX-PRISONERS WERE FORMED INTO A COMMANDO UNIT TO TACKLE SPECIAL MISSIONS. THEY FOILED A GERMAN ATTEMPT TO KIDNAP A GROUP OF BRITISH SCIENTISTS FROM AN ISLAND OFF THE COAST OF SCOTLAND, AND CAPTURED A NAZI U-BOAT WHICH HAD BEEN SENT TO COLLECT THE SCIENTISTS. LATER, THE BARBED-WIRE ELEVEN SAILED THE CAPTURED U-BOAT INTO A SCOTTISH SEAPORT...
HOOTS!
HOW ABOUT TRANSLATING FOR US, HAMISH!
OCH, 'TIS A BRAW SCOTTISH WELCOME THEY'RE GIVING US, LADDIES!
WHA' HAE!
U16
BRIGADIER SWEET MET THE TRIUMPHANT COMMANDOS ON THE QUAY...
GOOD SHOW, CHAPS! YOU'VE PROVED YOU CAN CARRY OUT A STICKY MISSION... NOW WE'VE GOT ANOTHER ONE LINED UP!
LEAD US TO IT, SIR!
FIRST YOU NEED SOME SPECIAL TRAINING! SERGEANT MAJOR MOOSE WILL TAKE CARE OF THAT!
OKAY, YOU GANGLING-GREENHORNS, GET THE LEAD OUT OF YOUR BOOTS!
CANADA
COR, THEY'VE PUT A CANADIAN IN CHARGE OF US!
THE TRUCK HEADED INTO THE SNOW-COVERED MOUNTAINS...
WHERE THE HECK IS THE MOOSE TAKING US?
BEGORRAH, MAYBE WE STEERED THAT U-BOAT TO LAPLAND BY MISTAKE!
OCH AWA', MIKE, 'TIS THE BONNY SCOTTISH HIGHLANDS, YE KEN!
AT LAST THEY TURNED INTO A GATEWAY...
ARMY WHAT SCHOOL?
SWOTTING?
SPYING?
SLEEPING, I HOPE!
ARMY
S NG
SCHOOL
THE ELEVEN HAD NO TIME TO INVESTIGATE THEIR SURROUNDINGS...
MAJOR FFOULKES AND PILOT OFFICER PLAYFAIR, YOU COME WITH ME!
WHAT ARE WE GOING TO DO HERE, SARN'T MAJOR?
YOU'RE GONNA MOVE, FELLA! INTO THAT DOORWAY THERE! MUSH!
INSIDE THE BUILDING...
COR, IT'S FREEZING IN HERE!
SOMEONE PUT THE LIGHTS ON!
RIGHT—GET FELL IN!

SUDDENLY, LIGHTS BLAZED...
ATTEN-SHUN!
B-BEDAD, BUT I'VE LEFT ME FEET BEHIND!
NO WONDER! THIS IS A SKATING RINK!
OCH, THEY'VE PUT THE BARBED-WIRE ELEVEN ON ICE!
OKAY, YOU TENDERFEET, MY JOB'S TO TEACH YOU ICE HOCKEY! BUT FIRST YOU'VE GOTTA LEARN TO SKATE!
I'LL SHOW THE SPALPEEN A THING OR TWO! 'TIS A DARLIN' SKATER I USED TO BE...
OH H-HECK!
...BUT... I'VE AFTER FORGOTTEN HOW TO PUT THE BRAKES ON!
HOOTS—MIKE! YOU'RE HEADING STRAIGHT FOR THE MOOSE...
S-SORRY, SARN'T MAJOR! 'TIS CARRIED AWAY I WAS!
GAAAAAR!
THEY'LL CARRY YOU AWAY ALL RIGHT, WISE GUY, WHEN I'VE FINISHED WITH YOU!
MIKE'S LEARNING FAST!
I WONDER WHAT KIND OF TRAINING THEY'RE GIVING MAJOR AND WINGS?
THE BARBED-WIRE ELEVEN HAD BEEN TAKEN TO A WINTER SPORTS RESORT, TAKEN OVER BY THE ARMY...
YOU MEAN WE'VE GOT TO LEARN TO SKI, CAPTAIN?
GLENGARRY WINTER SPORTS RESORT
ARMY SKIING SCHOOL
THAT'S RIGHT, MAJOR! AND YOU'VE GOT TO LEARN QUICKLY, SO...
UUR!
OOPS!
...OFF YOU GO! SORRY, CHAPS, BUT THIS IS A CRASH COURSE!
IT'S L-LIKE DIVING IN A SPITFIRE ... WITHOUT FLAPS OR A JOYSTICK!
WAAH! AND WE'RE G-GOING TO CRASH, ALL RIGHT!
OOOER!
IF WE SURVIVE THIS T-TRAINING, I WONDER WHAT KIND OF A C-CRAZY MISSION THEY HAVE COOKED UP FOR THE BARBED-WIRE ELEVEN THIS TIME?

NOW I'M GONNA SHOW YOU GREENHORNS HOW TO SKI! DON'T LOOK SO NERVOUS... THERE'S NOTHING DANGEROUS ABOUT SKI-ING!
OOER!
HUR, HUR! THAT'S WHAT HE THINKS!
GAAAR-OOOOF!
MAJOR FFOULKES AND WINGS PLAYFAIR HAD ALREADY TRIED THEIR HAND AT SKI-ING...
WHOOPS! S-SORRY, CHUM!
I'VE CHANGED MY MIND! TEACHING YOU HOW TO PLAY ICE-HOCKEY SHOULD BE LESS RISKY!
SKI-ING... ICE HOCKEY... WHAT KIND OF A MISSION ARE THEY SENDING US ON?
LATER, IN THE ICE RINK...
THE OBJECT OF THE GAME IS TO HIT THIS INTO YOUR OPPONENTS' GOAL!
M-MIGHT BE AN IDEA IF WE L-LEARNT TO SKATE FIRST!
HAMISH AND MIKE BOTH STARTED FORWARD...
BEGORAAAAH!
OCHHHHH!
PANDEMONIUM BROKE OUT...
H-HELP!
OWWW!
THE BRIGADIER WANTS TO KNOW IF THE BARBED-WIRE ELEVEN HAVE COMPLETED TRAINING, SERGEANT MAJOR!
YEAH! SURE! ANYTHING TO GET THOSE MISFITS OUTTA MY HAIR! TURN THEM LOOSE ON THE JERRIES, AND LET'S FINISH THE WAR!
I'LL LAY ON A TRUCK TO TAKE THEM TO THE AIRFIELD...

NEXT DAY, AT THE AIRFIELD...
GOOD SHOW, CHAPS! ALL SET FOR YOUR MISSION, ARE YOU? HOW WAS THE TRAINING?
ER...PAINFUL, BRIGADIER!
I KNOW THIS MISSION IS HUSH-HUSH, CHAPS, BUT THERE'S NO NEED TO DISGUISE YOURSELVES!
WE'RE NOT DISGUISED, SIR...WE'RE BANDAGED!
THE BRIGADIER GAVE A BRIEFING...
SOMEWHERE IN NORWAY, THE JERRIES HAVE HIDDEN A VITAL HEAVYWATER PLANT. WE'VE NO IDEA WHERE...BUT IT'S YOUR JOB TO LOCATE AND DESTROY IT!
JUST LIKE THAT, EH?
TO FOOL THE JERRIES, YOU'LL TRAVEL AROUND NORWAY DISGUISED AS A NEUTRAL ICE HOCKEY TEAM!
PHEW! LET'S HOPE NOBODY ASKS US TO PLAY ICE HOCKEY!
A FEW HOURS LATER, FAR ACROSS THE NORTH SEA...
THERE IT IS... OCCUPIED NORWAY... A HUNDRED THOUSAND SQUARE MILES OF SNOW, MOUNTAIN AND JERRIES!
...AND WE'VE GOT TO FIND ONE MEASLY LITTLE FACTORY, SOMEWHERE IN THE MIDDLE OF IT!
IT'S A TRICKY MISSION, CHAPS...BUT THAT'S WHY THEY CHOSE THE BARBED-WIRE ELEVEN TO TACKLE IT!
SURE AND WE'LL SKATE IT, BOYOS! AND I'M AFTER PRACTISING, SO I AM!
WATCH IT, MIKE! THOSE SKATES ARE SHARP... AND THE FUSELAGE IS ONLY MADE OF PLYWOOD...
B-BEDAD! NOW HE TELLS ME!
WEAKENED BY MIKE O'TOOLE'S ICE-SKATES, THE WHOLE FLOOR OF THE AIRCRAFT SPLIT OPEN...
BEJABBERS! 'TIS D-DROPPING OUT OF THE K-KITE, I AM!
OCH, WE'RE ALL GOING TO D-DROP OUT, THANKS TO THAT MUTTON-HEADED O'TOOLE!
INDEED TO GOODNESS, IT'S LUCKY WE'RE WEARING PARACHUTES!
BUT IF THE JERRIES ARE WAITING FOR US DOWN BELOW...OUR MISSION WILL BE OVER BEFORE IT'S STARTED!

AT THAT MOMENT...
LOOK OUT, SKIPPER! MOUNTAIN DEAD AHEAD!
WE MUST HAVE FLOWN OFF-COURSE, NEAR THE SWEDISH BORDER! NIP BACK AND TELL OUR PASSENGERS THEY WON'T BE JUMPING JUST YET!
BUT THE PASSENGERS HAD ALREADY GONE!
GALLOPING GREMLINS! THE FUSELAGE FLOOR'S DROPPED OUT...AND SO HAVE THE BARBED-WIRE ELEVEN!
LUCKILY THE ELEVEN HAD BEEN WEARING THEIR PARACHUTES...
NOT TO WORRY, CHAPS! WE'VE GOT TO START LOOKING FOR THAT HEAVYWATER PLANT SOMEWHERE!
AYE, BUT IT'LL NO' BE STUCK ON TOP OF THIS DIRTY GREAT MOUNTAIN.
URRRRGH!
OOOOOOSH!
OUT YOU COME, BOYO! 'TIS A SOFT LANDING WE MADE!
WE SEEM TO BE ON SOME KIND OF LEDGE ON THE MOUNTAINSIDE...WE'LL NEED OUR SKIS TO GET DOWN TO THE BOTTOM...
OCHH!
AND SO...
IT'S REAL STEEP—WE M-MIGHT BE MILES UP THE MOUNTAIN!
WE'LL SOON SEE, CHAPS...THE SNOW'S STOPPING...

THE COMMANDOS WERE ALREADY AT GROUND LEVEL!
SOME MOUNTAIN! WE'VE BEEN SKI-ING DOWN THE ROOF OF A BUILDING!
HOTEL
H-HUH?
B-BEGORRAH! THE CARPET'S STOPPING US, SO IT IS!
A NORWEGIAN HOTEL MANAGER GAPED AT THE VISITORS...
GREAT THOR! THEY MUST HAVE COME FROM SWEDEN, ACROSS THE MOUNTAIN! WHAT A FEAT OF SKI-ING!
OOER! LUCKY THE HOTEL DOOR'S OPEN!
HARSH VOICES GREETED THE ELEVEN...
WHO GAVE THESE SCHWEINHUNDS PERMISSION TO ENTER THE HOTEL WE HAVE COMMANDEERED?
DONNERWETTER!
OH, NO! JERRY BRASSHATS!
AHEM... WE ARE SWEDISH NEUTRALS, HERR GENERAL... COME TO MAKE AN ICE-HOCKEY TOUR OF NORWAY!
ACH SO! YOU ARE ICE-HOCKEY PLAYERS, HEIN? THAT IS SEHR GUT!
MAJOR FFOULKES TOLD THE COMMANDOS' COVER STORY...
COME THIS WAY...
I THINK HE'S ABOUT TO CALL OUR BLUFF!
TO THE ICE
THE DOORWAY LED TO AN INDOOR ICE RINK...
SEE, NEUTRALS? WE HAVE A GERMAN ICE-HOCKEY TEAM STAYING HERE...BUT THEY HAD NO-ONE TO PLAY UNTIL YOU ARRIVED!
WE'LL HAVE TO PLAY THIS TEAM, CHAPS, OR OUR COVER WILL BE BLOWN WIDE OPEN...
BUT WE CAN HARDLY SKATE, MAJOR... LET ALONE PLAY ICE-HOCKEY!
DISASTER THREATENED THE BARBED-WIRE ELEVEN!
ACHTUNG, NEUTRALS! YOU ARE READY TO START THE GAME?
GULP! LOOK AT THE SIZE OF THEM! WE'LL BE SLAUGHTERED!

KOMMEN, NEUTRALS! LET US GET ON WITH IT!
ULP! IT WON'T TAKE THEM LONG TO FIND OUT THAT WE CAN'T PLAY ICE HOCKEY!
NOR SKATE, EITHER!
AS THE ELEVEN DITHERED AT THE EDGE OF THE RINK...
WE'RE SUNK, CHAPS, BEFORE WE'VE EVEN STARTED OUR MISSION!
OCH, BUT I'VE A WEE IDEA FOR SINKING THE JERRIES, MAJOR! YOU STALL THEM WHILE I GET BUSY...
HAMISH MACTAVISH HURRIED OFF, FOLLOWED BY MIKE O' TOOLE...
SURE AND I HOPE YOU KNOW WHAT YOU'RE DOING, YE HAGGIS-BRAINED HIGHLANDER!
KONTROL
LET US WATCH THE MATCH FROM THE RINKSIDE, KAMERADEN! IT SHOULD BE VERY INTERESTING!
AS THE DISGUISED COMMANDOS WOBBLED ON TO THE ICE...
ACHTUNG! WHY HAVE YOU GOT NINE MEN OUT, NEUTRALS? DON'T YOU KNOW THAT THERE ARE ONLY SIX IN AN ICE-HOCKEY TEAM?
OH, CRUMBS, WE'VE MADE A MISTAKE ALREADY! HAMISH'S IDEA HAD BETTER BE A GOOD ONE!
MEANWHILE, IN A BACKROOM...
IT'LL TAKE A WEE BIT OF TIME FOR MY SCHEME TO WORK...
BEDAD, THEN I HOPE THE BOYOS CAN HOLD OUT THAT LONG WITHOUT GIVING THEMSELVES AWAY...
ON THE RINK...
WHAT'S THIS LITTLE ROUND RUBBER THING?
YOU HIT THAT, YOU TWIT!
SCHNELL! GET ON WITH THE GAME, NEUTRALS!
ER...WE'LL BE READY IN A MINUTE, HERR GENERAL!
BAGS I PLAY AT CENTRE!
GET LOST, COBBER, I'M PLAYING THERE!
KEEP STALLING, CHAPS!
DEAR ME, MY LACES HAVE COME UNDONE!

THE GERMAN TEAM WERE GETTING IMPATIENT...
ACH, DUMMKOPF! ARE YOU GOING TO PLAY ICE-HOCKEY, OR NOT?
ER...ULP...OF COURSE WE ARE... FINGERS CROSSED...
THERE'S NOTHING FOR IT, CHAPS...WE'VE GOT TO KICK OFF... I MEAN FACE OFF...
HAMISH'S IDEA COULDN'T HAVE BEEN SO HOT AFTER ALL...
HEY, I DON'T KNOW ABOUT THAT... LOOK AT THE ICE...
WATER WAS BUBBLING AROUND THE SKATES OF THE TWO TEAMS...
GREAT SCOTT! THE ICE IS MELTING!
H-HEIN?
D-DONNERWETTER!
YOU'RE DEAD RIGHT, JERRY...THE RINK'S GETTING WETTER AND WETTER!
HAMISH MUST HAVE REVERSED THE FREEZING APPARATUS!
NEIN, NEIN! I AM SINKING!
BEDAD, BUT YOU'RE A CANNY OLD SCOTSMAN, HAMISH, SO YOU ARE! 'TIS SAVED THE BARBED-WIRE ELEVEN YOU HAVE!
THE TWO TEAMS WERE SWIMMING NOW...
H-HILFE...GLUG!
HOW ABOUT MAKING IT A GAME OF WATER POLO, JERRIES! WE'RE GOOD AT THAT!
WHAT A PITY WE CAN'T PLAY ICE-HOCKEY WITH YOUR TEAM, HERR GENERAL!
JA, NEUTRAL! IT WILL TAKE HOURS TO FREEZE THE RINK AGAIN, AND MY GERMAN PLAYERS MUST RETURN TO DUTY...
MAJOR FFOULKES ASKED A SEEMINGLY INNOCENT QUESTION...
THEY'RE SOLDIERS ARE THEY, HERR GENERAL?
JA! THEIR JOB IS TO GUARD A TOP-SECRET FACTORY TWENTY MILES FROM HERE!
HEAR THAT, CHAPS? COULD BE THAT TOP-SECRET FACTORY IS THE HEAVY-WATER PLANT WE'RE LOOKING FOR!
SO WHEN THE JERRIES LEAVE HERE, MAJOR... WE'LL SHADOW THEM!

LATER...
BE SURE YOU GUARD THE TOP-SECRET FACTORY WELL, WHEN YOU RETURN TO DUTY, MEN!
ALL WE'VE GOT TO DO IS FOLLOW THEM, MAJOR!
SOUNDS EASY, WINGS... BUT WHAT DO WE USE FOR TRANSPORT?
MIKE O' TOOLE AND HAMISH MACTAVISH HAD BEEN SEARCHING SOME OUTBUILDINGS...
SURE AND HOW ABOUT THESE?
TURN IT UP, COBBERS... THERE'S ELEVEN OF US, REMEMBER!
ALORS! CHIPS AND I HAVE FOUND SOMETHING...
IS JUST THE JOB, NO?
I'LL BE DARNED... A VINTAGE SLEIGH!
BUT IT TOOK EIGHT OF THE ELEVEN TO MOVE THE SLEIGH!
PITY YOU DIDN'T FIND A HORSE AS WELL, FROG!
HUH, I THOUGHT THERE'D BE A SNAG IN IT!
WE'VE LOST SIGHT OF THE JERRIES, CHAPS... CAN'T YOU PULL A BIT FASTER?
URRH... YOU MUST BE JOKING!
BEDAD! LOOK AHEAD, BOYOS!
HOORAY! THE ROAD'S SLOPING DOWNWARDS!
ALL ABOARD, BLOKES!

GOOD-OH, NOW WE'RE REALLY SHIFTING!
HMM, THE ROAD'S GETTING A BIT STEEP, ISN'T IT?
AND THERE'S A HEAP OF HAIRPIN BENDS AHEAD...
THE MAJOR SUDDENLY THOUGHT OF SOMETHING!
ER, NONE OF YOU CHAPS NOTICED A BRAKE ON THIS THING, HAVE YOU?
N-NO, MAJOR! CAN'T SAY I HAVE!
'TIS OVER THE EDGE WE'LL BE GOING!
HELP!
THE RUNAWAY SLEIGH FLIRTED WITH DISASTER AT EVERY HAIRPIN BEND...
BUT THEIR LUCK HELD...
ACHTUNG!
PHEW! THANK GOODNESS, THAT WAS THE LAST BEND!
AND THERE'S THE JERRY TRUCK AHEAD!
OH, NO! WE'VE DONE BETTER THAN FOLLOW THE JERRIES... WE'RE OVERTAKING THEM!
HEIN? IT IS THE NEUTRAL ICE-HOCKEY TEAM!
THEN DISASTER STRUCK!
ACH! LOOK OUT, YOU DUMMKOPFS!
S-SORRY, JERRIES! THEY FORGOT TO PUT A STEERING WHEEL ON THIS CONTRAPTION!
AAAACH!
OWWWW!
THE GERMANS BOILED WITH RAGE...
GRRRRCH!
SCHWEINHUNDS!
ACH, CALL YOURSELVES NEUTRALS, DO YOU? I SUSPECT THAT YOU ARE ENEMIES! AND I HAVE WAYS OF FINDING OUT!
OH DEAR! I'M AFRAID THIS SNOW ISN'T COOLING THE JERRIES DOWN!

ACHTUNG! YOU SEE THE FROZEN LAKE DOWN THERE, NEUTRALS? YOU WILL NOW GIVE A SKATING DISPLAY ON IT, ONE BY ONE!
WE WILL SOON SEE WHETHER YOU ARE REALLY ICE-HOCKEY PLAYERS... OR IMPOSTORS! YOU FIRST, DUMMKOPF!
OH, NO!
MAJOR FFOULKES TRUDGED UNHAPPILY OFF.
SCHNELL!
ULP! MUST I?
GOSH, WE'VE HAD IT NOW, BLOKES!
THE MAJOR CAN'T SKATE FOR TOFFEE-NUTS... AND HE'S BEST OF THE LOT OF US!
THE JERRIES ARE BOUND TO TWIG US!
BUT!
ACH, SO! MOST IMPRESSIVE!
HEY—LOOK, YOU BLOKES—THE MAJOR'S SKATING PERFECTLY!
WHAT'S COME OVER HIM?
YOUR CAPTAIN IS OBVIOUSLY A SKILLED SKATER, NEUTRALS! NOW YOU TWO WILL DEMONSTRATE YOUR TALENTS!
OH HECK, MIKE AND HAMISH ARE SURE TO FALL FLAT ON THEIR FACES!
BUT ONCE AGAIN...
I DON'T BELIEVE IT! THEY'RE PUTTING ON A FANTASTIC SHOW!
THEY'RE SKATING LIKE CHAMPS!
ACH, IT SEEMS WE MISJUDGED YOU, NEUTRALS! BUT LET US SEE ONE MORE OF YOU DEMONSTRATE YOUR SKILL!
DON'T WORRY, CRUSHER... EVERYTHING'S ORGANISED...

WHEN CRUSHER REACHED THE EDGE OF THE ICE, HIDDEN FROM THE GERMANS...
MEET SOME NORWEGIAN PALS OF OURS, CRUSHER! THE MAJOR FOUND THEM HIDING FROM THE JERRIES HERE, AND THEY OFFERED TO HELP US!
HUH?
ONE OF THE NORWEGIANS BORROWED CRUSHER'S JACKET...
YOU MEAN...IT WAS THEM WE SAW SKATING ON THE ICE?
SURE IT WAS, BOYO! FOINE STAND-INS THEY MAKE, DON'T THEY?
WOW! LOOK AT OLD CRUSHER DOING HIS STUFF!
WUNDERBAR!
GOSH, WE'VE SURE FOOLED THE JERRIES!
WE OWE YOU AN APOLOGY, NEUTRALS!
JA, JA! YOU ARE BRILLIANT SKATERS!
AS A FAVOUR, WOULD YOU AND YOUR SKILFUL COMRADES COME TO OUR SECRET FACTORY TO GIVE US A SKATING LESSON?
GOSH, YES! WE'D BE GLAD TO!
TEN MINUTES LATER, THE ELEVEN'S SLEIGH THEY HAD "BORROWED" WAS HITCHED TO THE GERMAN TRUCK...
WE'RE TAKING A RISK, AREN'T WE, MAJOR, GOING WITH THE JERRIES?
MAYBE...BUT IT'S A PERFECT CHANCE FOR US TO INFILTRATE THAT SECRET FACTORY THEY'RE GUARDING!
COULD BE IT'S THE HEAVYWATER PLANT WE'VE GOT TO LOCATE AND DESTROY!
OCH, 'TIS A PITY WE DIDNA BRING THOSE NORWEGIAN TYPES ALONG! THEY'RE RESISTANCE FIGHTERS AND EXPLOSIVE EXPERTS, YE KEN!
HOW DO YOU KNOW, HAMISH?
OCH, THEY TOLD ME! AND I SAW A COUPLE OF THEM SABOTAGING THE JERRY TRUCK WHILE THE REST OF US WERE WATCHING THE SKATING!
HAMISH IS RIGHT, MAJOR! LOOK—THERE'S A BOMB TAPED UNDER THE TRUCK!
OH, NO! IF IT EXPLODES – IT'LL BLOW THE LOT OF US TO SMITHEREENS!

WE'VE GOT TO STOP THAT BOMB EXPLODING, CHAPS...OR WE'LL BE BLOWN UP, AS WELL AS THE JERRIES!
LEAVE IT TO ME, SPORT...
THE AUSTRALIAN, BLUEY MILLER, CLIMBED ALONG THE TOW CHAIN...
GOSH! D'YOU THINK YOU CAN REACH THE BOMB, BLUEY?
IF I CAN'T COBBER, START WORRYING!
HEIN? WHAT ARE YOU DOING, KAMERAD?
SAVING US ALL A LOAD OF GRIEF, SPORT! YOU'RE SITTING ON A BOMB!
THEN...
BUT THAT'S GOT RID OF IT!
HOORAY! NICE WORK, BLUEY!
ACH, WE ARE SAVED!
THE BOMB SAILED THROUGH THE AIR...
LOOK! WE HAVE ARRIVED AT THE SECRET FACTORY IT IS OUR JOB TO GUARD!
OH HECK! AND THE BOMB'S GOING TO ARRIVE THERE AS WELL, ANY MOMENT NOW!
NAZI MINISTRY OF INVENTIONS TOP SECRET, EINGANG VERBOTEN
AAAARGH!
HILFE!
ACHTUNG! WE ARE UNDER ATTACK! RETURN THE ENEMY'S FIRE!
THE FACTORY GUARDS OPENED FIRE...
THE ATTACKERS ARE USING ONE OF OUR OWN GERMAN TRUCKS, MEN! BLAST IT TO PIECES!
ACH, I AM COVERED IN SNOW!

GOSH, OLD BLUEY'S REALLY STARTED SOMETHING!
DON'T THEY KNOW WE'RE NEUTRALS?
THEIR OWN PALS ARE COPPING IT, TOO!
HALTEN YOUR FIRE, YOU DUMMKOPFS!
THAT'S IT, JERRY, YOU TELL 'EM!
ACHTUNG! THERE HAS BEEN A MISTAKE! IT IS OUR OWN KAPITAN OUTSIDE THE GATES!
THE EXPLOSION WAS CAUSED BY A TIME-BOMB, HERR COLONEL, WHICH WAS PLANTED ON OUR TRUCK BY PARTISANS! THESE NEUTRALS DISCOVERED THE BOMB AND SAVED OUR LIVES!
ACH, SO?
THE COLONEL WAS A SUSPICIOUS TYPE...
THE NEUTRALS ARE AN ICE-HOCKEY TEAM FROM SWEDEN, HERR COLONEL!
SWEDEN, HEIN? I WILL TELEPHONE OUR NAZI EMBASSY THERE, AND CHECK THEIR CREDENTIALS!
OH, NO...
IT WON'T TAKE THAT FAT NAZI LONG TO TWIG THAT WE'RE FAKES...SO WE'VE GOT TO WORK FAST! WE MUST FIND OUT WHETHER THIS IS THE HEAVYWATER PLANT WE'VE COME TO DESTROY!
LET'S TAKE A LOOK IN THIS SHED, TAFF...
CRUSHER AND TAFF STEPPED INSIDE THE SHED....
LOOKS LIKE SOME KIND OF DRESSING ROOM. SIX UNIFORMS... SIX PAIRS OF SKIS...SIX OF EVERYTHING...
BUT NO SIGN OF THE SIX JERRIES IT ALL BELONGS TO...
TAFF PEERED INSIDE AN INNER DOOR...
BRRR! WE SHAN'T FIND THE SIX JERRIES IN HERE, THAT'S FOR SURE! IT'S LIKE A GIANT REFRIGERATOR....WITH A MINI-SNOWSTORM THROWN IN!
MUST BE SOME KIND OF EXPERIMENTAL CHAMBER... WHERE THEY TEST THINGS IN ARCTIC CONDITIONS...
LOOK, CRUSHER! IT'S NOT THINGS THEY TEST IN HERE...'TIS MEN!
BLOW ME DOWN, IT'S THE SIX JERRIES THAT GEAR BELONGED TO! THEY'RE MARCHING ROUND AND ROUND IN THE FREEZING COLD!
BUT...THEY'RE CAKED FROM HEAD TO FOOT IN ICE!

WE'VE GOT TO GET THESE POOR BLOKES OUT OF HERE, TAFF, BEFORE THEY FREEZE TO DEATH!
'TIS ICED UP TO THE EYEBROWS THEY ARE!
TAFF AND CRUSHER DRAGGED TWO OF THE STRANGE FIGURES OUT OF THE TEST-CHAMBER...
COME IN TO THE WARM, BACH!
Y'KNOW IT'S A FUNNY THING, TAFF... BUT THEIR ARMS AND LEGS ARE MOVING AS IF THEY WERE STILL MARCHING!
THEN...
LOOK YOU, CRUSHER, THEY ARE STILL MARCHING!
THE ICE IS MELTING OFF THEIR BODIES! WHAT KIND OF MEN ARE THEY?
OOER! THEY'RE NOT MEN AT ALL... THEY'RE ROBOTS!
YOU GO AND TELL THE OTHERS, CRUSHER! I'LL STAY HERE!
OUTSIDE, IN THE YARD OF THE SECRET FACTORY...
HEY, MAJOR!
SSH, CRUSHER! HE'S TRYING TO KEEP THE JERRY COLONEL FROM FINDING OUT THAT WE'RE NOT A NEUTRAL ICE-HOCKEY TEAM!
THE JERRY'S RINGING SWEDEN TO CHECK ON US... AND THE MAJOR'S INTERCEPTED THE CALL BY PLUGGING A HANDSET INTO THE TELEPHONE CABLE!
JA, JA, HERR COLONEL! THIS IS DER GERMAN EMBASSY IN STOCKHOLM SPEAKING!
MAJOR FFOULKES WAS SPEAKING GERMAN, IN A DISGUISED VOICE...
HIMMEL! IT SOUNDS AS THOUGH YOU ARE JUST OUTSIDE MY WINDOW!
HA, HA! THE HERR COLONEL WILL HAVE HIS LITTLE JOKE! NOW WHAT CAN I DO FOR YOU!

CONTINUED ON PAGE 81

MANY of Britain's top sports photographers contribute to your action-packed TIGER Annual . . . and we have selected what we consider to be six of their best pictures. Jumping straight in with the action, is this superb telephoto shot of West German show jumping star Hendrick Snoek on his horse Palma Nova. More of 'Six of the Best' over the page.

Six of the Best!

Everton played in two Cup Finals in 1984. They lost to Liverpool in the Milk Cup Final, but two months later they beat Watford 1-0, in the F.A. Cup Final . . . hence the photo above! Below, England's Karl Tatham tries to avoid 'Czech-mate' in a basketball match against Czechoslovakia!

An outstanding photo of America's Phil Mahre seen on the way to winning the Men's Slalom gold medal at the 1984 Winter Olympics in Sarajevo, Yugoslavia. Phil's brother Steven made it a family 'double' by winning the silver medal!

Wild water canoeing certainly lives up to its name as you can see from this superb photo, above, of Britain's Andy Dovey battling in a sea of surf! This photo of Marc Surer crashing in the Dutch Grand Prix certainly made an impact — it didn't do the car much good, either!

RACING TO SUCCESS!

Michelin House in London provides a historic display of scenes from the early days of cycling and motoring. Here is Charles Terront on his way to victory in the 1891 Paris to Brest and back cycle race.

The Michelin Brothers Edouard and Andre proving that pneumatic tyres worked well on the horseless carriage in the 1895 Paris to Bordeaux and back car race.

Many of the world's top cyclists, rally drivers, motor racers and motorcycle stars have benefitted from the expertise of one of the top tyre manufacturers — Michelin. Here is a brief history of the company's road to racing success. We hope you find it interesting.

The Michelin brothers, Andre and Edouard started in the tyre business by using sport to promote their new products. They wanted the whole world to 'ride on air', that is on the pneumatic tyre which is so well known today.

In 1891 the first long distance cycle race was organised, from Paris to Brest and back, a distance of 750 miles. Other people used pneumatics, but when they had punctures, they took a long time to repair. The Michelin tyre was easily removed and replaced. The Michelin rider Charles Terront, won the race by 8 hours and completed the distance in 3 days and nights — with no sleep. Michelin cycle tyres were suddenly in huge demand.

In 1895, the first race was organised, from Paris to Bordeaux and back, for the great new invention — the motor car. None of the car makers would fit Michelin air filled tyres, they all preferred solid rubber tyres, so the

Michelin brothers built 3 cars themselves. Only one car got to the starting line in Paris, it was called L'Eclair (Lightning) not for its rapid progress, but the way it zig-zagged from side to side! The car was driven by the brothers and, despite many breakdowns, they finished the 750 mile race and proved 'pneumatic tyres' worked well on the horseless carriage!

Progress was rapid. Cars became faster. The first ever grand prix, the 1906 French Grand Prix was won by Szisz in a Renault on Michelin tyres. Michelin dominated racing until 1912, when they stopped competing because the tyres used on racing cars were too different from those on normal cars.

Two World Wars passed before Michelin returned to competition, and in the mid-1960s development started on motorsport tyres, again to prove a point. The radial tyres, developed by Michelin in 1948 had not been tested at high speeds. Motor sport provided an ideal test bed.

8 YEARS OF MICHELIN IN THE FORMULA ONE WORLD CHAMPIONSHIP

	Michelin Wins	Number of Races
1977	0	17
1978	5	16
1979	7	15
1980	3	15
1981	13	15
1982	8	16
1983	9	15
1984	14	16

Rallying was the first area to receive attention and the great success of the Alpine Renaults in 1971, 72, 73 and 74 owed a lot to Michelin tyres.

In 1977, Michelin entered Formula One with Renault, to test the radial tyres in the highest possible level of competition. Michelin also equipped Ferrari in 1978, and one year later, in 1979, Jody Scheckter won the Worl Championship on Michelin.

After 8 successful seasons in Formula One, Michelin have withdrawn for similar reasons to 1912, the Grand Prix tyres are now too different from normal tyres, and what a note to finish, with 14 out of 16 Grands Prix in 1984 won on Michelin, and Niki Lauda in a McLaren the World Champion.

MICHELIN AND MOTOR SPORT

Left, Niki Lauda in a McLaren, racing to the chequered flag in the 1984 British Grand Prix and his 3rd World Championship title. Szisz in a Renault wins the first Grand Prix, the French Grand Prix at Sarthe in 1906, below.

Above, an Alpine-Renault 1600S in the 1971 Monte Carlo Rally on Michelin Tyres, bringing the Tyre Company back to motor sport. Left, Jody Scheckter in a Ferrari on his way to victory in the 1979 Drivers' Championship in Formula One.

The Audi Quattro of Stig Blomqvist showing the masterful form which won him the 1984 World Rally Championship.

Michelin is now concentrating more and more on rallying. The 1984 season saw success in the World Rally Championship for Stig Blomqvist in an Audi Quattro. While in Britain, Scotland's Jimmy McRae, won the home championship in his Michelin-shod Opel Manta 400.

The 1985 World Championship rally scene, sees many new 4 wheel drive specials. Tony Pond driving Austin Rover's MG Metro 6R4 will be preparing for the 1986 season. Favourite for the 1985 title was Ari Vatanen in the Peugeot 205 T16, which clearly won the 1984 RAC Rally. Ari made a brilliant start to the 1985 World Rally Championship by winning the 53rd Monte Carlo Rally, with Michelin-tyred cars taking the first 5 places.

On two wheels Michelin have dominated motorcycle sport for nearly 10 years. Britain's Barry Sheene, who announced his retirement in 1985, won his 1976 and 1977 World Championship titles on Michelin, as did many other famous names. Let's hope that new generations of motor sport stars will be racing to success on Michelin tyres for many years to come!

Scotsman Jimmy McRae, below, raising the dust in his home rally to win the British Championship Title. Right, Tony Pond driving the MG Metro 6R4 on its debut in the forests of Yorkshire.

MICHELIN AND MOTOR SPORT

Left, Britain's Barry Sheene, on a Yamaha – a master on 2 wheels. Below, Ari Vatanen making a splash on his way to victory in the 1984 RAC Rally, in the 4 wheel drive Peugeot.

Meet one of Britain's most glamorous sports stars — world water ski champion Liz Hobbs!

Water Ski-

Photo left: Liz poses by the 500 horse power engines that nearly dragged her to her doom. But, amazingly, she was back on her skis less than seven weeks after the accident, intent on defending her European title that she won in 1982.

Liz lost the European title in 1984, but was determined to retain her World Water Ski Racing title in September 1985. Here, she poses with the £25,000 tow boat, and although travelling at over 70 m.p.h., photo far right, Liz still manages a smile for our cameraman! What a super girl!

But shortly after these photos were taken, Liz nearly lost her life in a fall which left her being dragged at 80 m.p.h. behind the tow boat driven by her father. She broke her breast-bone, six ribs and a foot.

...ing Super Girl!

KEEP ON TRUCKIN'!

A NEW form of Grand Prix racing came to Britain in a 'big' way in 1984 — in trucks! Donington Park race circuit was the venue for the debut of these mighty juggernauts — and provided great action!

America and Europe have held truck racing events for some years, but this was the first time that the 'giants of the road' had been let loose on a British race track. The turbo-charged, diesel-engined monsters are all road-going vehicles — indeed, the winning driver had hauled a trailer of goods from Italy, unhitched it, won the race and then took another cargo back! It's like a motorway rush-hour, photo above, as the trucks roar away from the start! Hurling a vehicle weighing between 5 and 7½ tons around the circuit at speeds up to 100 m.p.h. is quite a challenge . . . and one that former motorcycle racer Barry Sheene could not resist! Barry, seen right, with his lucky number 7, drove his DAF into appropriately 7th place! More races are planned for Britain — so keep on truckin', fellers!

An extra thrill for the 100,000 spectators, was the amazing stunt-display by the Bataille family from France. You've probably seen car-balancing on two wheels . . . but a five-ton truck, photo below, is nothing short of incredible and brings a whole new meaning to the word 'tyre-pressures'!

Nose to tail racing in vehicles costing around £40,000 is hairy stuff . . . but fortunately accidents are rare.

ROMA PAY THE PENALTY...

WHEN Liverpool met A.S. Roma in the 1984 European Cup Final at Rome's Olympic Stadium, the Anfield Reds were bidding for their fourth triumph in the competition. Phil Neal, the only survivor of the side that gave Liverpool their first European Cup in 1977, opened the scoring with this superbly-taken goal, photo sequence above. Roma equalised just before half time, but after

extra time, the sides were still deadlocked 1-1. So the Cup was to be decided in a penalty shoot-out. Steve Nicol hit 'Pool's first penalty wide, but then Roma missed two spot kicks. Now it was all up to Alan Kennedy, photo left. The left back made no mistake, photo below, and minutes later, skipper Graeme Souness, right, was thankfully raising the trophy. Phew, but it had been close!

. . . AND LIVERPOOL WIN THE CUP!

NOT OUT!

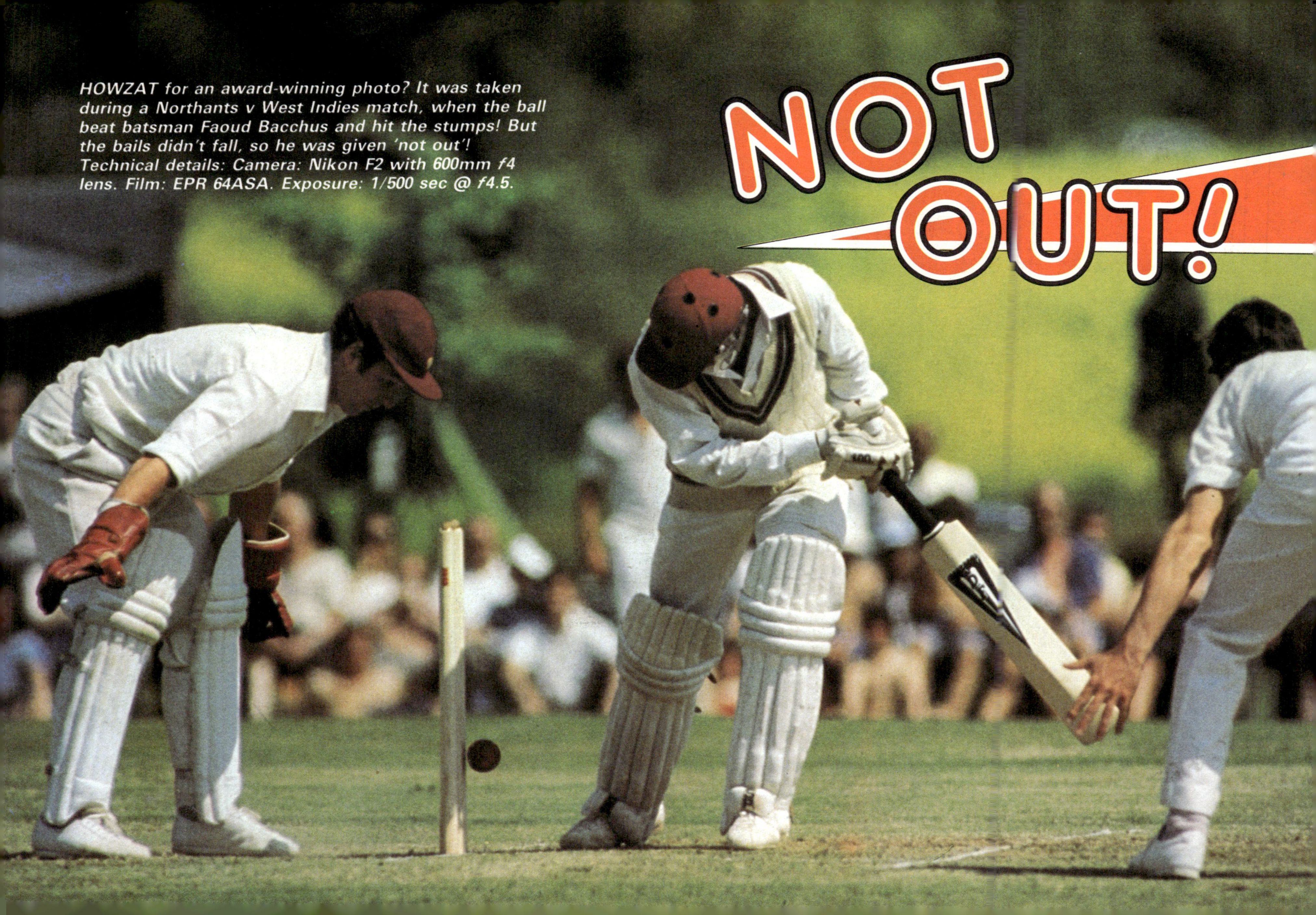

HOWZAT for an award-winning photo? It was taken during a Northants v West Indies match, when the ball beat batsman Faoud Bacchus and hit the stumps! But the bails didn't fall, so he was given 'not out'! Technical details: Camera: Nikon F2 with 600mm *f4* lens. Film: EPR 64ASA. Exposure: 1/500 sec @ *f4.5*.

THE BARBED-WIRE X1
CONTINUED FROM PAGE 64
YOU WANTED TO KNOW IF MY ROBOTS COULD BE PROGRAMMED TO PLAY ICE-HOCKEY, EH? WELL THERE IS YOUR ANSWER!
TERRIFIC! I SAY, YOU'RE NOT A GERMAN, ARE YOU?
THE INVENTOR SPOKE PROUDLY TO MAJOR FFOULKES...
ME, GERMAN? NEVER! I AM A NORWEGIAN PATRIOT! THE NAZIS HAVE TAKEN OVER THESE ROBOTS I HAVE INVENTED, BUT I SHALL FIND A WAY TO OUTWIT THEM!
MAYBE WE CAN HELP YOU THERE...
WE'RE BRITISH COMMANDOS DISGUISED AS A NEUTRAL ICE-HOCKEY TEAM... THE JERRIES WANT A MATCH, BUT WE CAN'T PLAY!
SO YOU WILL BE UNMASKED, EH... UNLESS MY ROBOTS CAN TAKE YOUR PLACES?
RELAX, THEN, BRITISHERS! WITH THIS REMOTE-CONTROL BOX, I CAN MAKE MY ROBOTS DO ANYTHING...
BEGORRAH, 'TIS A PLEASURE TO MEET YOU, BOYOS!
WE'RE SAVED, CHAPS! WE'LL DRESS UP THESE MECHANICAL MARVELS TO LOOK LIKE US...AND THE ROBOTS CAN PLAY THAT ICE-HOCKEY MATCH AGAINST THE JERRIES!
LATER...
ACHTUNG! WE ARE READY TO BEGIN THE GAME, HERR COLONEL...
SEHR GUT! WE WILL SEE WHETHER THESE NEUTRALS ARE THE CRACK PLAYERS THEY CLAIM TO BE!
THE MAJOR WAS WATCHING WITH THE NAZI COMMANDANT, COLONEL SCHMURK...
WHERE IS YOUR TEAM, NEUTRAL?
ER...THEY'RE JUST ABOUT TO SKATE OUT, HERR COLONEL...I HOPE...

THE ROBOTS GLIDED ON TO THE ICE...
YES! THERE THEY ARE NOW!
PHEW. WHAT A RELIEF!
HIMMEL, THESE NEUTRALS LOOK GOOD!
CONTROL!
NILS, THE INVENTOR, WAS HIDDEN INSIDE A HUT NEARBY...
HAW! IF ONLY THE JERRIES KNEW THOSE ROBOTS OF YOURS ARE REALLY CONTROLLED,
YOU HAVE SEEN NOTHING YET, MY FRIENDS...
NEXT MOMENT, THE ROBOTS SWEPT INTO ACTION...
DONNERWETTER!
THE NEUTRALS ARE SKATING RINGS ROUND US!
AAAGH!
GOAL! HOW'S THAT FOR A START, HERR COLONEL?
HIMMEL! THESE NEUTRALS OF YOURS ARE CERTAINLY SKILLED!
NICE WORK, NILS! WE COULDN'T HAVE DONE BETTER OURSELVES!
SSH, BOYOS! THERE'S A COUPLE OF JERRIES WALKING PAST OUTSIDE!
ACHTUNG, FELDWEBEL! GO TO THE TEST-SHED AND SEE HOW THE NORWEGIAN INVENTOR IS GETTING ON WITH HIS ROBOTS!
OH, NO...
I MUST HURRY TO THE TEST-SHED AND HEAD OFF THAT GERMAN, OR ALL WILL BE LOST! TAKE THE REMOTE-CONTROL BOX, FRIEND!
M-ME? B-BUT I CAN'T H-HANDLE THOSE ROBOTS OF YOURS!
SOMEBODY'S GOT TO REMOTE-CONTROL THE ROBOTS, WINGS! HURRY UP, THEY'RE READY FOR THE FACE-OFF!
ULP, ALL RIGHT! I'LL PRESS THIS BUTTON AND HOPE FOR THE BEST...
OH, CRUMBS! YOU'VE MADE THE ROBOT WALLOP THE REF, WINGS! NOW THERE'LL BE TROUBLE...
AAAACH!

ACH! HIT THE REFEREE, WOULD YOU? I AM SENDING YOU OFF FOR A TEN-MINUTE PENALTY!
THAT'S TORN IT!
WINGS PLAYFAIR WAS TRYING TO REMOTE-CONTROL THE ROBOTS FROM A HUT BESIDE THE RINK...
GET THAT ROBOT OFF THE ICE, WINGS, OR THE JERRIES WILL GUESS IT'S NOT US OUT THERE!
I DON'T KNOW WHICH BUTTON IS WHICH, CHAPS! I'LL PUSH THE LOT AND HOPE FOR THE BEST!
HIMMEL! NOW THE OTHER NEUTRALS ARE CLOSING IN ON ME FROM ALL SIDES!
OCH! STOP THOSE CRAZY CONTRAPTIONS, WINGS, BEFORE THEY CAUSE A RIOT!
H-HILFE! THE NEUTRALS ARE GOING TO ATTACK ME!
BEGORRAH! 'TIS DONE IT NOW YOU HAVE, WINGS, BOYO!
MAJOR FFOULKES AND FOUR OF HIS MEN WERE WATCHING FROM THE STAND...
B-BLITZEN!
SOMETHING'S GONE WRONG, CHAPS. THOSE ROBOTS HAVE BLOWN THEIR TOPS! WE MUST GET OUT THERE AND STOP THEM!
ACH! THE NEUTRALS ARE GOING BERSERK! SEND THEM ALL OFF!
QUICK, CHAPS! WE'LL HAVE TO GO ON AS SUBSTITUTES!
3
INSIDE THE HUT...
OCH, 'TIS A WONDER THE JERRIES HAVENA' TWIGGED THEY'RE PLAYING ROBOTS, AND NOT US!
I'VE SWITCHED THE CONTROL-BOX RIGHT OFF, CHAPS! THAT'S THAT!

AS THE ROBOTS' POWER WAS SWITCHED OFF...
ACH, NOW THE NEUTRALS ARE COLLAPSING!
A GOOD THING TOO, EH, MAJOR? THE MECHANICAL MONSTROSITIES NEARLY GAVE THE GAME AWAY!
THE GERMAN COMMANDANT WAS FURIOUS
DRAG THE ROBOTS OFF THE ICE, CHAPS!
MORE TROUBLE FROM THESE DUMMKOPF NEUTRALS AND I WILL PUT THEM ALL UNDER ARREST!
PROP THEM UP IN THE PENALTY BOX, CHAPS! WE MAY NOT PLAY ICE-HOCKEY AS WELL AS THEY CAN, BUT AT LEAST WE WON'T BREAK THE RULES!
I'D LIKE TO KNOW WHERE THAT NORWEGIAN BOFFIN'S GOT TO!
THE NORWEGIAN INVENTOR WAS HURRYING TOWARDS THE ICE RINK...
SCHNELL, YOU NEUTRAL SUBSTITUTES! LET US RESTART THE GAME!
PHEW, PANIC OVER!
DON'T SPEAK TOO SOON, CRUSHER! HERE COMES NILS...AN HE LOOKS ALL OF A TWITTER!
MORE TROUBLE, MY FRIENDS! THE GERMANS WISH TO INSPECT MY ROBOTS, WHICH ARE SUPPOSED TO BE PERFORMING IN THE TEST-SHED!
OH, GOSH! IF THEY FIND OUT THE ROBOTS ARE AT THE ICE RINK, WE'LL BE SUNK!
THERE IS ONLY ONE WAY OUT, ENGLISHMEN...YOU WILL HAVE TO TAKE THE PLACE OF MY ROBOTS!
ULP! YOU MEAN WE'VE GOT TO ACT AS SUBSTITUTES FOR THEM?
A FEW MINUTES LATER...
DUMMKOPF! YOU TOOK LONG ENOUGH TO OPEN THE DOOR!
ER, YES, BUT... AHEM... THERE ARE MY ROBOTS, ALL PRESENT AND CORRECT!
THE GERMANS WERE IMPRESSED BY THE SIX FIGURES...
SEHR, GUT! THE ROBOTS MARCH SMARTLY, HEIN?
JA, JA, HERR LEUTNANT! ONE WOULD ALMOST THINK THEY WERE HUMAN!
PHEW! LOOKS AS THOUGH WE'VE FOOLED THE JERRIES, EH, WINGS?
YES, BUT THEY'RE IN NO HURRY TO GO...AND... HOW LONG CAN WE KEEP UP THIS ROBOT ACT?

VERY INTERESTING! YOUR ROBOTS LOOK ALMOST HUMAN, NORWEGIAN! LET US SUBJECT THEM TO SOME TOUGHER TESTS!
N-NO! DO NOT PUNCH THEM — THEY ARE VERY...ER, SENSITIVE, YOU KNOW!
THE "ROBOTS" GROANED INWARDLY!
I'LL SAY WE'RE SENSITIVE!
LET'S HOPE THOSE JERRIES DON'T GET ANY MORE BRIGHT IDEAS ABOUT TESTING US!
ACH SO. HERR LEUTNANT, PERHAPS WE COULD SET OFF ONE OF THESE FLAME-CANISTERS AND SEE IF THE ROBOTS ARE FIREPROOF!
NEIN, YOU MIGHT DAMAGE THEM! I WILL TURN ON THE HEATING FULL BLAST, AND SEE HOW THAT AFFECTS THEIR MACHINERY!
AS THE TEST-SHED WARMED UP...
OH HECK, IT'S GETTING LIKE AN OVEN IN HERE! AND IF THE JERRIES NOTICE WE'RE PERSPIRING, THEY'LL GUESS WE'RE NOT ROBOTS!
I'VE GOT AN IDEA! WHY DON'T WE PRETEND THE HEAT HAS MADE US GO OUT OF CONTROL?
I GET YOU, CRUSHER! BRILLIANT IDEA! COME ON...
H-HIMMEL! TWO OF THE ROBOTS ARE ADVANCING ON US... PERHAPS THEY ARE GOING BERSERK?
B-BLITZEN! YOUR OBSERVATION WAS CORRECT, FELDWEBEL-AAAACH!
GNNNNK!
GOOD ON YOU, CRUSHER! WHEN THE JERRIES WAKE UP, THEY'LL THINK IT WAS THE ROBOTS WHO CLOBBERED THEM!
SURE AND WHY DON'T THE ROBOTS WRECK THE WHOLE FACTORY WHILE THEY'RE ABOUT IT?

TERRIFIC IDEA, MIKE! TAKE A FIRE-CANISTER EACH, CHAPS, AND PRETEND YOU'RE ROBOTS ON THE RAMPAGE!
TEST SHED
ACHTUNG! THE ROBOTS HAVE GOT OUT OF THE TEST SHED!
JA, AND THEY ARE SETTING FIRE TO THE FACTORY! THEIR CONTROLS MUST HAVE BROKEN DOWN!
FLAMES WERE SOON SPREADING RAPIDLY...
SCHNELL! WE MUST INFORM THE HERR COLONEL OF THIS DISASTER!
WE'VE FOOLED THE JERRIES, CHAPS! THEY THINK IT'S THE ROBOTS WHO ARE SABOTAGING THEIR FACTORY!
THE NAZI COMMANDANT HAD BEEN WATCHING THE ICE-HOCKEY MATCH NEARBY...
THE ROBOTS HAVE GONE HAYWIRE, HERR COLONEL! THEY ARE BURNING DOWN OUR FACTORY!
H-HEIN?
THE FIVE OTHER COMMANDOS OF THE BARBED-WIRE ELEVEN HAD BEEN PLAYING IN THE MATCH...
ACHTUNG! STOP THE GAME! THE FACTORY IS ON FIRE! WE MUST SAVE IT FROM DESTRUCTION AT THE HANDS OF THE ROBOTS!
WHAT'S HE TALKING ABOUT, MAJOR? THE ROBOTS ARE SITTING IN THE PENALTY BOX OVER THERE, WHERE WE LEFT THEM!
WHEN THE GERMANS HAD GONE...
HI, MAJOR! THE LADS AND ME HAVE WRECKED THE PLACE...AND PUT ALL THE BLAME ON THE ROBOTS!
I'LL BE DARNED! WELL, I RECKON THIS IS OUR CHANCE TO MAKE OURSELVES SCARCE, BEFORE THEY FIND OUT THEIR MISTAKE!
I SHALL ESCAPE WITH MY ROBOTS INTO THE MOUNTAINS, WHERE MY FELLOW-PATRIOTS CAN USE THEM AGAINST THE GERMANS!
AND WE'D BETTER GET ON WITH OUR SEARCH FOR THE HEAVYWATER PLANT!
THE ELEVEN COMMANDEERED A TRUCK...
CAREFUL, CHAPS! WE DON'T WANT THE JERRIES TO SPOT US!
THEY'RE TOO BUSY TRYING TO SAVE THEIR FACTORY TO TAKE ANY NOTICE OF US, MAJOR!
THEY'RE WASTING THEIR TIME! IT'S A WRITE-OFF!
WELL WE'VE CAUSED THE JERRIES A FAIR BIT OF TROUBLE ALREADY –
YES, GOOD SHOW, CHAPS! BUT IT'S THE SECRET HEAVYWATER PLANT WE CAME TO NORWAY TO DESTROY...AND BELIEVE ME, IT'S GOING TO TAKE SOME FINDING!

HOURS LATER...
HEY, LOOK AT THAT SMOKE RISING FROM THE TOP OF THAT MOUNTAIN! I DIDN'T KNOW THEY HAD VOLCANOES IN NORWAY!
THEY DON'T, WINGS! THIS NEEDS LOOKING INTO!
THERE'S A CHAIN OF BUCKETS, TOO, GOING DOWN THE MOUNTAINSIDE TO THAT SHIP IN THE FIORD!
COULD BE THE JERRIES HAVE GOT A SECRET FACTORY ON TOP OF THE MOUNTAIN, CHAPS! DRIVE DOWN TO THE QUAY, BLUEY!
THE STEEP ROAD TO THE FIORD WAS TREACHEROUS WITH ICE...
OCH, AYE... TAKE YOUR FOOT OFF THE ACCELERATOR, BLUEY MON! WE'RE GOING INTO A SKID!
THE BRAKES AND THE WHEEL HAVE PACKED UP! I CAN'T STOP!
BEDAD, WE'RE SKIDDING TOWARDS THE BUCKET CHAIN, SO WE ARE!
THE CAB OF THE TRUCK HIT ONE OF THE DANGLING BUCKETS...
INDEED TO GOODNESS, THE BUCKETS ARE FULL OF WATER! WE'RE GOING TO GET A DRENCHING!
UURGH!
THAT WATER REALLY HURTS!
IT SURE SEEMS HEAVIER THAN ORDINARY WATER!
OCCCH!
OWWWW!

SMITHY HAD A SMATTERING OF SCIENTIFIC KNOW-HOW...
THEY'RE RIGHT, MAJOR! IT LOOKS LIKE ORDINARY WATER, BUT I'D SAY ITS DENSITY WAS TEN PER CENT HIGHER...AND THAT MEANS IT ACTUALLY IS DEUTERIUM OXIDE....OR HEAVYWATER!
THE STUFF FROM THE SECRET PLANT WE CAME TO NORWAY TO DESTROY!
BUT MINUTES LATER...
ACHTUNG! ARREST THOSE DUMMKOPFS IN THE TRUCK!
BUT THE BARBED-WIRE ELEVEN HAD BEEN BUSY!
THOSE JACKETS DRAPED ROUND EACH SACK AND FIXED ON SKIS MIGHT JUST FOOL THE JERRIES!
THE GERMANS SAW THE BULKY SHAPES SLIDING AWAY FROM THE TRUCK...
ACH SO! THE SCHWEINHUNDS ARE TRYING TO ESCAPE ON SKIS! AFTER THEM!
WE SHALL SOON CATCH THEM...THEY SKI LIKE SO MANY SACKS!
OUR DODGE WORKED, CHAPS...BUT WE'VE GOT NO TIME TO WASTE...
MAJOR FFOULKES JUMPED FROM THE ROOF OF THE CAB...
FOLLOW ME!
HUH? YOU MEAN WE'RE GOING FOR A RIDE IN A BUCKET?
THERE'S NO QUICKER WAY TO REACH THE TOP OF THE MOUNTAIN!
IF MY HUNCH IS CORRECT, CHAPS, WE'LL FIND WHAT WE'VE BEEN LOOKING FOR UP AT THE MOUNTAIN TOP!
SURE AND 'TIS THE LAST PLACE YOU'D EXPECT TO FIND A FACTORY...
AS THE BUCKETS REACHED THE TOP...
OCH, YOU WERE RIGHT, MAJOR!
IT'S THE SECRET HEAVYWATER PLANT!
NOW ALL WE'VE GOT TO DO IS BLOW THE PLACE UP!
BEGORRAH! BUT FIRST, I'M THINKING WE'D BETTER MAKE SURE WE'RE NOT DROWNED IN A BUCKETFUL OF HEAVYWATER!

HEY! WHY ARE YOU TIPPING THE BUCKET OVER, MIKE?
'TIS EITHER THAT, MAJOR, OR WE'LL BE UP TO OUR EYES IN HEAVYWATER, SO WE WILL!
THE ELEVEN HAD LANDED INSIDE THE SHED WHERE THE BUCKETS WERE FILLED WITH HEAVYWATER...
YOU'VE GOT SOMETHING THERE, MIKE! AND WE'LL MAKE SURE ALL THE BUCKETS STAY EMPTY WHILE WE'RE BLOWING UP THE FACTORY!
HOW DO WE MANAGE THAT, MAJOR?
ANGELLINO AND FROG WILL SHOW YOU HOW, WINGS! THEY'RE DEAD-SHOTS WITH THEIR TOMMY-GUNS!
I GET IT, BOSS! AIM AT THE BUCKETS, FROG!
ALORS! WHAT DO YOU ENGLISH SAY... ZERE IS A HOLE IN MY BUCKET?
PHEW! THIS'LL FETCH THE JERRIES RUNNING!
SURE ENOUGH...
ACHTUNG! SABOTEURS! SHOOT THE SCHWEINHUNDS!
GOOD-OH! I WANTED TO DRAW THE JERRY GUARDS OUT OF THE SECRET PLANT!
THE BARBED-WIRE ELEVEN BLAZED INTO ACTION...
THE REST OF YOU KEEP THE JERRIES BUSY, WHILE WINGS AND I PLANT THE TIME-BOMBS!
AAAGH!
BUT...
WE WILL GET A GOOD FIELD OF FIRE FROM HERE, FRANZ!
CLOBBER THE SQUAREHEADS, BLOKES!
H-HIMMEL!

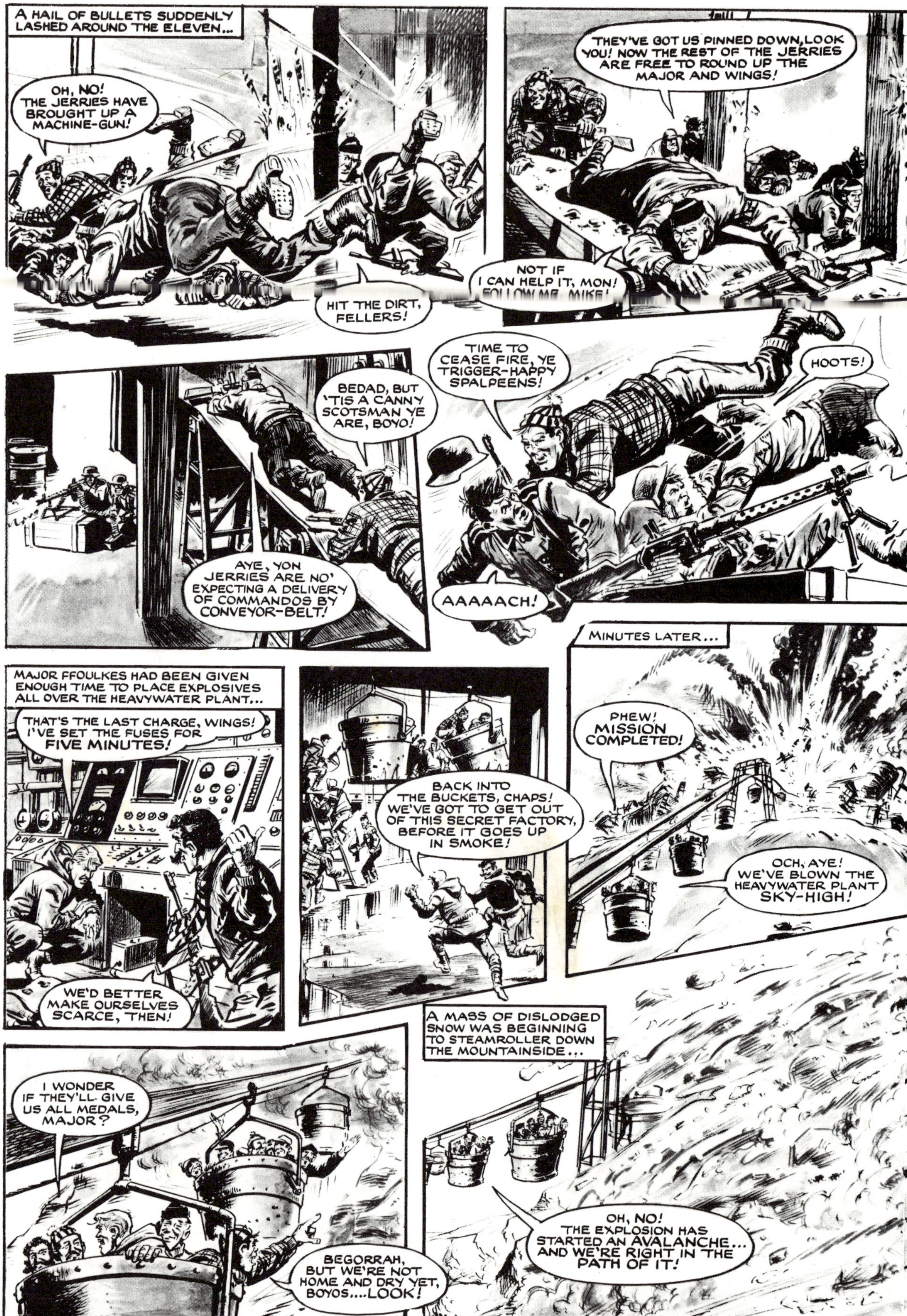
A HAIL OF BULLETS SUDDENLY LASHED AROUND THE ELEVEN...
OH, NO! THE JERRIES HAVE BROUGHT UP A MACHINE-GUN!
HIT THE DIRT, FELLERS!
THEY'VE GOT US PINNED DOWN, LOOK YOU! NOW THE REST OF THE JERRIES ARE FREE TO ROUND UP THE MAJOR AND WINGS!
NOT IF I CAN HELP IT, MON! FOLLOW ME, MIKE!
BEDAD, BUT 'TIS A CANNY SCOTSMAN YE ARE, BOYO!
AYE, YON JERRIES ARE NO' EXPECTING A DELIVERY OF COMMANDOS BY CONVEYOR-BELT!
TIME TO CEASE FIRE, YE TRIGGER-HAPPY SPALPEENS!
HOOTS!
AAAAACH!
MAJOR FFOULKES HAD BEEN GIVEN ENOUGH TIME TO PLACE EXPLOSIVES ALL OVER THE HEAVYWATER PLANT...
THAT'S THE LAST CHARGE, WINGS! I'VE SET THE FUSES FOR FIVE MINUTES!
WE'D BETTER MAKE OURSELVES SCARCE, THEN!
BACK INTO THE BUCKETS, CHAPS! WE'VE GOT TO GET OUT OF THIS SECRET FACTORY, BEFORE IT GOES UP IN SMOKE!
MINUTES LATER...
PHEW! MISSION COMPLETED!
OCH, AYE! WE'VE BLOWN THE HEAVYWATER PLANT SKY-HIGH!
I WONDER IF THEY'LL GIVE US ALL MEDALS, MAJOR?
BEGORRAH, BUT WE'RE NOT HOME AND DRY YET, BOYOS....LOOK!
A MASS OF DISLODGED SNOW WAS BEGINNING TO STEAMROLLER DOWN THE MOUNTAINSIDE...
OH, NO! THE EXPLOSION HAS STARTED AN AVALANCHE... AND WE'RE RIGHT IN THE PATH OF IT!

IT'S TOO LATE TO MAKE A RUN FOR IT, CHAPS! THIS IS OUR LAST MISSION!
FROM THEIR TWO BUCKETS, THE BARBED-WIRE ELEVEN AWAITED THE END...
OCH AYE, 'TIS SMASHED TO SMITHEREENS, WE'LL BE!
THAT'S RIGHT, HAMISH, CHEER US UP!
OWWW! THE WHOLE THING'S COLLAPSED!
SO LONG, CHAPS! IT'S BEEN NICE KNOWING YOU!
HEY, WAIT A MOMENT, MAJOR...
THE BUCKETS ARE SLIDING DOWN ON TOP OF THE AVALANCHE LIKE SLEDGES!
'TIS BETTER THAN TOBOGGANING!
BUT WHAT HAPPENS WHEN WE REACH THE BOTTOM?

WE'RE SLIDING RIGHT ACROSS THE JETTY!
HECK, AND THAT'S A JERRY SHIP WE'RE
THE TWO BUCKETS CAREERED ON UNCHECKED...
YIKES–NOW WE'RE SLIDING CLEAN ACROSS THE SHIP!
H-HIMMEL!
...AND INTO THE SEA!
OCH! DINNA SAY WE'VE ESCAPED THE AVALANCHE...ONLY TO GET DROWNED!
OUR LUCK'S STILL IN, BLOKES...THE BUCKETS ARE FLOATING!
AND THAT'S MORE THAN YOU CAN SAY FOR YON JERRY SHIP, LOOK YOU...
IT'S TURNING TURTLE UNDER THE WEIGHT OF THE AVALANCHE!
...AND TAKING THE LAST OF JERRY'S HEAVYWATER TO THE BOTTOM WITH IT!
WE'VE WELL AND TRULY COMPLETED OUR MISSION, CHAPS!
THREE CHEERS FOR THE BARBED-WIRE ELEVEN! HIP-HIP... HOORAY!
THE GERMANS ON SHORE SOON RECOVERED FROM THEIR SHOCK...
CURSE THE BRITISH SABOTEURS! THEY WILL PAY FOR THIS! LAUNCH THE LONGBOAT, KAMERADEN!
LOOK, MAJOR... THE JERRIES ARE ON THE WAR-PATH!
HMM, WE'RE IN A SPOT, CHAPS! THESE BUCKETS FLOAT ALL RIGHT... BUT YOU CAN'T GO PLACES IN THEM...
BEGORRAH, BUT THE SEA IS BUBBLING ROUND US, SO IT IS!
A WEIRD NEW PERIL THREATENED THE BARBED-WIRE ELEVEN...
SOMETHING IS RISING FROM THE SEA, RIGHT UNDERNEATH US!
IT COULD BE A M-MONSTER!

BEGORRAH! 'TIS A WHALE, SO IT IS!
BUT, MIKE, WHALES AREN'T MADE OF STEEL! IT'S A SUBMARINE!
PHEW, WHAT A RELIEF! IT'S A BRITISH SUBMARINE, TOO!
WE SAW THE EXPLOSION, CHAPS, AND GUESSED IT WAS YOU BLOWING UP THE HEAVYWATER FACTORY! CLIMB ABOARD!
NEXT DAY, THEY REACHED AN ENGLISH COASTAL TOWN...
HOORAY FOR THE BARBED-WIRE ELEVEN!
RA-RA-RA!
I'LL BET THE JERRIES LOCKED UP IN THAT PRISON CAMP ON CASTLE HILL CAN HEAR THE CHEERING!
THE TRIUMPHANT COMMANDOS DROVE PAST THE CAMP...
ACHTUNG! THEY SAY YOU ENGLANDERS ARE CRACK FOOTBALLERS! WE CHALLENGE YOU TO PLAY OUR GERMAN PRISONERS' TEAM!
PRISON CAMP FOR GERMAN P.O.Ws! KEEP OUT
TCHAH! OUT OF THE QUESTION!
SO... THE ENGLANDERS ARE SCARED!
THE DUMMKOPFS KNOW THEY WOULD GET BEATEN!
I ABSOLUTELY FORBID THE ELEVEN TO PLAY FOOTBALL AGAINST THOSE JERRY PRISONERS!
THOSE JERRIES AREN'T GOING TO SNEER AT US, CHAPS! WE'LL PLAY THEM, EVEN IF IT MEANS WE'VE GOT TO BREAK INTO THEIR PRISON CAMP!
NEXT DAY...
COME ON, CHAPS... LET'S TAKE A LOOK ROUND THE LOCAL MUSEUM...
MUSEUM
GOOD SHOW! I'M GLAD THOSE HOTHEADS HAVE FORGOTTEN ABOUT A FOOTBALL MATCH AGAINST THE JERRIES!

BUT IN THE MUSEUM BASEMENT...
I DID SOME INVESTIGATING, CHAPS...AND DISCOVERED THERE WAS THIS SECRET TUNNEL WHICH LEADS INTO THE CASTLE PRISON CAMP!
THE ELEVEN FILED ALONG THE TUNNEL...
MAKES A CHANGE, DOESN'T IT BLOKES... BURSTING INTO A PRISON CAMP INSTEAD OF OUT OF ONE!
OCH AYE, AND A PRISON CAMP FOR JERRIES, AT THAT!
WHEN THEY FINALLY EMERGED...
WE'VE COME TO PLAY THAT SOCCER MATCH AGAINST YOU, JERRIES! DON'T TELL THE CAMP GUARDS, WILL YOU?
HIMMEL! IT IS THE BARBED-WIRE ELEVEN!
NEIN, ENGLANDERS, WE WILL KEEP THE MATCH A SECRET! AND FRITZ WILL GUARD YOUR CLOTHES WHILE YOU PLAY!
THE ELEVEN CHANGED INTO SOCCER STRIP...
JA JA! THE UNIFORMS OF THE BARBED-WIRE ELEVEN ARE MOST VALUABLE, HEIN?
THE MATCH STARTED...
I WONDER WHY THE JERRIES SEEM SO GLAD TO HAVE US IN THEIR CAMP, MAJOR?
I RECKON THEY'RE HOPING TO LICK US, WINGS... BUT WE LL SHOW THEM HOW TO PLAY SOCCER!
THE BRITISH CAMP GUARDS SUSPECTED NOTHING...
I DIDN'T KNOW THE JERRIES HAD TWO CRACK SOCCER TEAMS IN THE CAMP, TOSH!
THE NEW PLAYERS ARE HOT STUFF, WHOEVER THEY ARE!
SOON...
AAAACH!
GOAL!
SPOT ON, BLUEY!
THE GERMAN SPECTATORS RUSHED ON TO THE PITCH, CHEERING...
WUNDERBAR!
HOORAY!
I'LL BE DARNED! THEY SEEM GLAD WE'VE SCORED IT DOESN'T MAKE SENSE!
DARK DOUBTS SUDDENLY ASSAILED THE BARBED-WIRE ELEVEN!
H-HEY, WHAT'S GOING ON, MAJOR?
OUCH! I'VE GOT A NASTY SUSPICION THAT THEY'RE NOT JUST CONGRATULATING US, CHAPS... THEY'RE CLOBBERING US!

I DON'T KNOW WHO THOSE NEW SOCCER PLAYERS ARE, BUT THEY SEEM MIGHTY POPULAR WITH THE JERRIES!
LOOK—THEY'RE BEING MOBBED BY THE OTHERS!
BUT THE GERMANS WERE USING THEIR FISTS ON THE BARBED-WIRE ELEVEN!
OUCH!
UURF!
MAJOR, WE ARE BEING CLOBBERED!
THE ELEVEN WERE VICTIMS OF A CUNNING PLAN...
THE BRITISCHERS ARE KAPUT, HERR KAPITAN!
SEHR GUT! LOCK THEM IN ONE OF THE HUTS, WHILE WE DRESS UP IN THEIR UNIFORMS!
OUR PLAN HAS WORKED WELL, KAMERADEN! NOW WE CAN USE THE SECRET TUNNEL TO ESCAPE FROM THE PRISON CAMP...POSING AS THE BARBED-WIRE ELEVEN!
THE DISGUISED GERMANS DIVED INTO THE SECRET TUNNEL...
DRESSED IN THE BRITISCHERS' UNIFORMS, IT WILL BE SIMPLE FOR US TO COMMANDEER A BOAT AND SAIL BACK TO GERMANY!
MEANWHILE, THE ELEVEN WERE LOCKED IN A PRISON HUT...
OH LUMME, WE'RE REALLY IN THE SOUP NOW!
CHEER UP, CHAPS, WE'RE SUPPOSED TO BE EXPERT ESCAPERS! THE FIRST THING IS TO GET FREE FROM THESE ROPES!
LOOK, FROG'S BOUNCING UP AND DOWN!

FROG LANDED ON THE NEXT BED...
OOF! WHAT'S THE BIG IDEA?
WAKE UP, CHIPS! NOW YOU CAN REACH MY ROPES AND UNTIE ME!
THE JERRIES MUST HAVE PINCHED OUR UNIFORMS TO ESCAPE IN, MAJOR!
THEY WON'T GET FAR ONCE WE'VE GIVEN THE ALARM!
I'LL NIP STRAIGHT TO THE MAIN GATE, AND TELL THE GUARDS WHO WE ARE AND WHAT'S HAPPENED!
HMM... THE WAY WE'RE DRESSED IN JERRY PRISONER GEAR, I HOPE THEY BELIEVE YOU!
MINUTES LATER...
I TELL YOU WE'RE THE BARBED-WIRE ELEVEN!
COME OFF IT, JERRY! THOSE DON'T LOOK LIKE BRITISH COMMANDO UNIFORMS YOU'RE WEARING!
BACK TO YOUR HUTS, SQUAREHEADS!
BUT YOU'RE LETTING THE JERRIES ESCAPE!
COME ON, COBBERS, WE'RE NOT GOING TO TALK OUR WAY OUT OF THE PRISON CAMP!
BLUEY BELIEVED IN ACTION...
SO LET'S START BY UPENDING THESE DUSTMEN!
SORRY, BOYOS, WE NEED YOUR DUST-CART!
ALL ABOARD, SPORTS!
LIKE OLD TIMES, ISN'T IT?
SURE IS, EXCEPT THAT NOW WE'RE BUSTING OUT OF A BRITISH PRISON CAMP!
HEY! WHAT ARE THOSE JERRIES UP TO IN THE DUSTCART?
OH, NO! THE CHAPS WILL NEVER GET AWAY WITH THIS!
STAND BY TO PICK UP THE MAJOR AND WINGS, COBBERS! THEN WE'LL BULLDOZE OUR WAY OUT OF THE MAIN GATES!

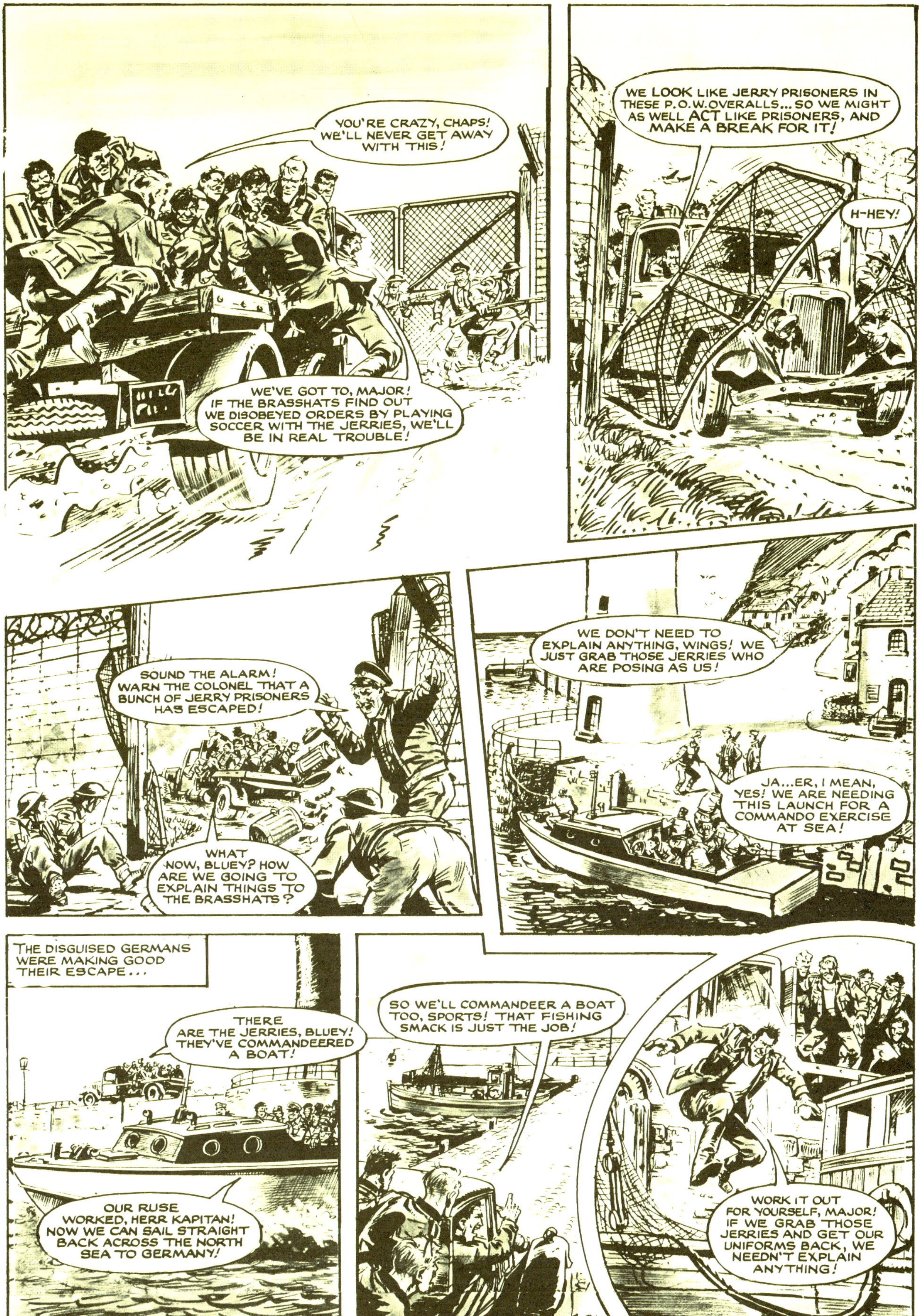
YOU'RE CRAZY, CHAPS! WE'LL NEVER GET AWAY WITH THIS!
WE'VE GOT TO, MAJOR! IF THE BRASSHATS FIND OUT WE DISOBEYED ORDERS BY PLAYING SOCCER WITH THE JERRIES, WE'LL BE IN REAL TROUBLE!
WE LOOK LIKE JERRY PRISONERS IN THESE P.O.W. OVERALLS... SO WE MIGHT AS WELL ACT LIKE PRISONERS, AND MAKE A BREAK FOR IT!
H-HEY!
SOUND THE ALARM! WARN THE COLONEL THAT A BUNCH OF JERRY PRISONERS HAS ESCAPED!
WHAT NOW, BLUEY? HOW ARE WE GOING TO EXPLAIN THINGS TO THE BRASSHATS?
WE DON'T NEED TO EXPLAIN ANYTHING, WINGS! WE JUST GRAB THOSE JERRIES WHO ARE POSING AS US!
JA...ER, I MEAN, YES! WE ARE NEEDING THIS LAUNCH FOR A COMMANDO EXERCISE AT SEA!
THE DISGUISED GERMANS WERE MAKING GOOD THEIR ESCAPE...
THERE ARE THE JERRIES, BLUEY! THEY'VE COMMANDEERED A BOAT!
OUR RUSE WORKED, HERR KAPITAN! NOW WE CAN SAIL STRAIGHT BACK ACROSS THE NORTH SEA TO GERMANY!
SO WE'LL COMMANDEER A BOAT TOO, SPORTS! THAT FISHING SMACK IS JUST THE JOB!
WORK IT OUT FOR YOURSELF, MAJOR! IF WE GRAB THOSE JERRIES AND GET OUR UNIFORMS BACK, WE NEEDN'T EXPLAIN ANYTHING!

IF WE GRAB THE JERRIES, BLUEY! THAT LAUNCH OF THEIRS IS A LOT FASTER THAN THIS OLD TUB!
BLUEY TOOK A HEADER OFF THE BOWS...
NOT TO WORRY, COBBERS! I KNOW HOW TO STOP THE JERRIES' BOAT!
THE AUSTRALIAN SWAM UNDERWATER, TRAILING A NET FROM THE FISHING SMACK BEHIND HIM...
WITH A SHUDDER, THE LAUNCH'S ENGINE STOPPED...
HIMMEL! A FISHING NET HAS TANGLED ITSELF ROUND OUR PROPELLER!
GOOD-OH, NOW THE JERRIES ARE SITTING DUCKS!
NEXT MOMENT...
ALL ABOARD, BLOKES!
WE'LL TEACH THE SQUAREHEADS TO PULL A FAST ONE ON US!
THE GERMANS WERE NO MATCH FOR THE ELEVEN...
K-KAMERAD!
H-HILFE!
TAKE OUR UNIFORMS OFF THE JERRIES, SPORTS, AND WE'LL GIVE THEM BACK THEIR PRISON TOGS!
A FEW MINUTES LATER...
IT LOOKS AS THOUGH THE BARBED-WIRE ELEVEN HAVE MANAGED TO RECAPTURE THOSE ESCAPED PRISONERS, SIR!
YOU WERE RIGHT, BLUEY! WE'VE GOT AWAY WITH IT!
GOOD SHOW, MAJOR FFOULKES! IT'S LUCKY YOU AND YOUR CHAPS HAPPENED TO BE AROUND WHEN THOSE JERRIES ESCAPED!
WITH THE HELP OF THE BARBED-WIRE ELEVEN I HAVE NO DOUBTS THAT WE WILL WIN THE WAR!

"DOCTOR, THOSE TABLETS YOU GAVE ME TO STOP ITCHING HAVEN'T WORKED!"
"THEN, WE'LL HAVE TO START FROM SCRATCH AGAIN!"
"DOCTOR, I FEEL LIKE A KANGAROO!"
"YOU MUSTN'T JUMP TO CONCLUSIONS!"
"DOCTOR, I FEEL LIKE A BOAT!"
"IT'S ALL RIGHT YOU'RE IN SHIP-SHAPE CONDITION!"
"DOCTOR, I FEEL LIKE A PACKET OF BUTTER, WHAT CAN IT BE?"
"I DON'T KNOW, BUT LET'S HOPE IT DOESN'T SPREAD!"
"DOCTOR! I FEEL LIKE A POGO STICK!"
"I'M SORRY, SIR, BUT YOU CAN'T JUMP THE QUEUE!"
DOCTOR DOCTOR...
X-RAY DEPT.
"HOW'S YOUR BAD FOOT?"
CHIROPODIST
"THEN WHEN I BLEW FOR A GOAL, THEY ALL CAME AND PATTED ME ON THE BACK!"
"TAKE THREE TEASPOONS OF THIS MEDICINE DAILY!"
"BUT WE'VE ONLY GOT TWO TEASPOONS AT HOME!"

Twenty years may have gone by, but a tall, dark-haired centre-forward named Hateley is still knocking in the goals. Back in the 1960s, Tony Hateley was a much-travelled striker who was lethal in the air. He is pictured on this page playing for Liverpool. And in the 1980s, son Mark, an AC Milan player, is flying the flag for the Hateleys and England. Top right, Mark gets into the action for England v Finland. Bottom right, he scores during the same game. Dad never played for his country, but he's thrilled about his son's success.

LIKE FATHER...

...LIKE SON!

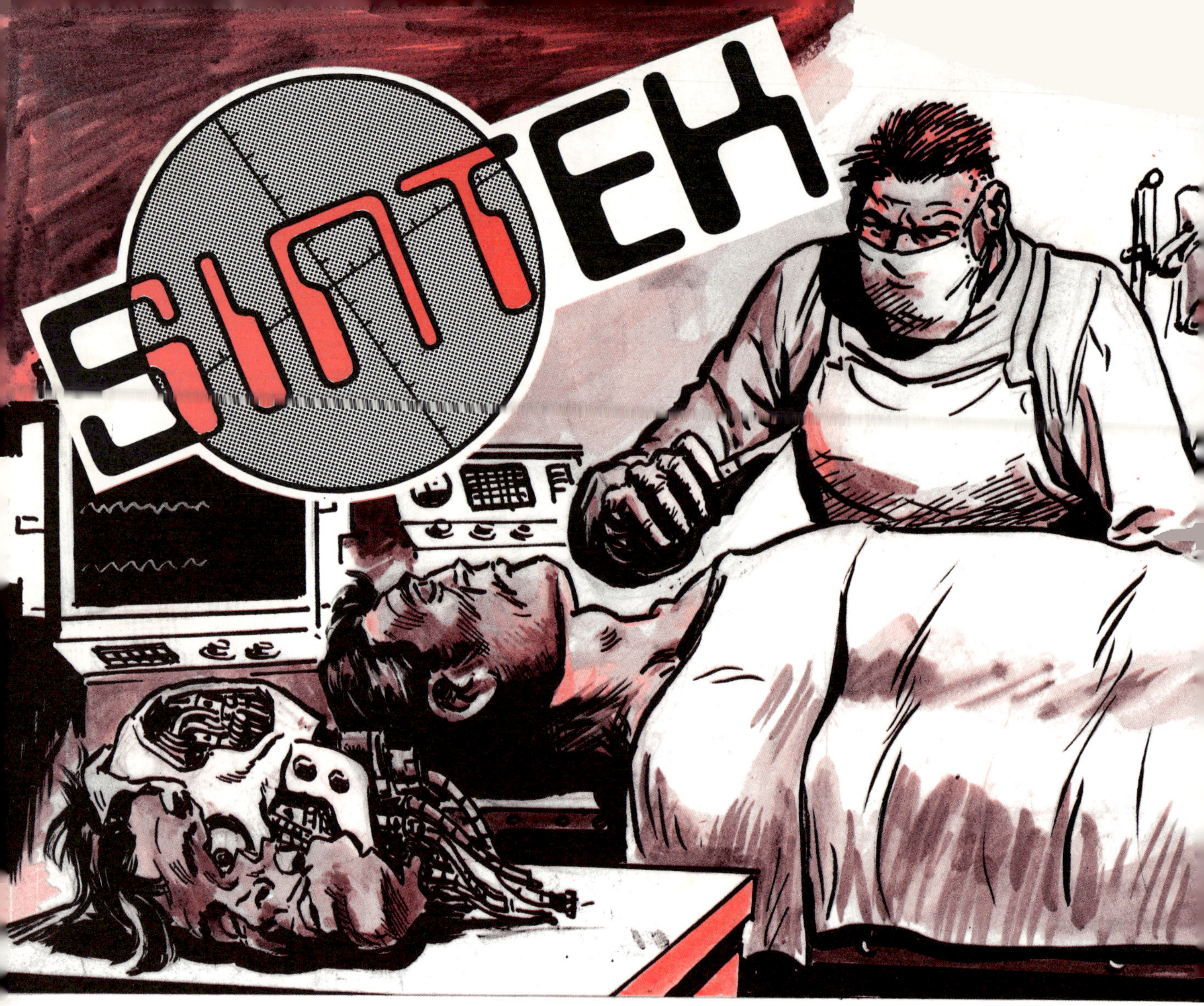

TWO-THIRTY A.M. in the Science Department of the University of California. There was a faint 'click' as a piece of plastic tripped the lock on the door of the exhibits room.

Rubber-soled feet crept silently along a line of glass cases, until they halted in front of a cabinet containing a gruesome-looking specimen — a man's head!

The intruder drew in his breath sharply. He'd been told what to look for, but coming face to face with the blank, unseeing eyes in the semi-darkness almost made him turn and run.

Then, his courage renewed with the thought of the five hundred dollars he was being paid for the night's work, he grabbed the head and hastily stuffed it in the holdall he carried.

Outside on the campus, Barney Coleman's lean, muscular figure moved stealthily from building to building, taking advantage of all the shadows. He knew the layout of the place by heart; after all, he'd been a student at the university for three years. Captain of the football and basketball teams! After failing his medical exams, he'd turned to crime!

"Strange," he thought to himself, "the head hadn't felt human, more like plastic!"

A car glided up to the university gates as he shinned to the ground.

"Did you get it?" hissed the driver, urgency in his voice.

"Yeah, sure thing, Mister Weltmann," replied Barney. "Though it beats me why you want the horrible object!"

"Fancy yourself as a bit of a Doctor Frankenstein, do you?" joked Barney as he got into the car's rear seat.

"Yes, something like that," answered the driver, his eyes narrowing as he reached for a control on the dashboard.

A glass partition slid noiselessly into position, isolating the rear compartment.

"Hey, what's going on?" yelled Barney, beating on the glass with his fists.

The driver smiled as he watched through the rear-view mirror.

"You're going to make a great contribution to science, my friend!" he murmured, as a cloud of gas seeped through the loudspeaker grilles to envelop his victim.

The car sped on its way through empty, suburban roads, before turning into a private drive. Electronically-operated gates responded to the touch of a button, gliding silently apart.

As the vehicle stopped in front of a large mansion, a white-coated figure appeared pushing a trolley.

"Is everything okay?" he asked the driver.

"Yes . . . Coleman's in a coma. Get him to the laboratory quickly and on to a respirator," came the reply in a heavy Austrian accent.

Taking the holdall from the car's rear seat, the driver went into the house and entered a library, whose shelves were crammed with medical and scientific books.

He unwrapped the head and examined it carefully. A mass of wires dangled from the neck where it had been severed from what once had been a living body!

"So, we meet at last, Sintek!" he gloated, placing the bizarre object on a small table.

Gunter Weltmann sat back contentedly and his mind returned to the events of six months ago. Of how his brilliant scientist brother, Anton, had held America to ransom with an army of

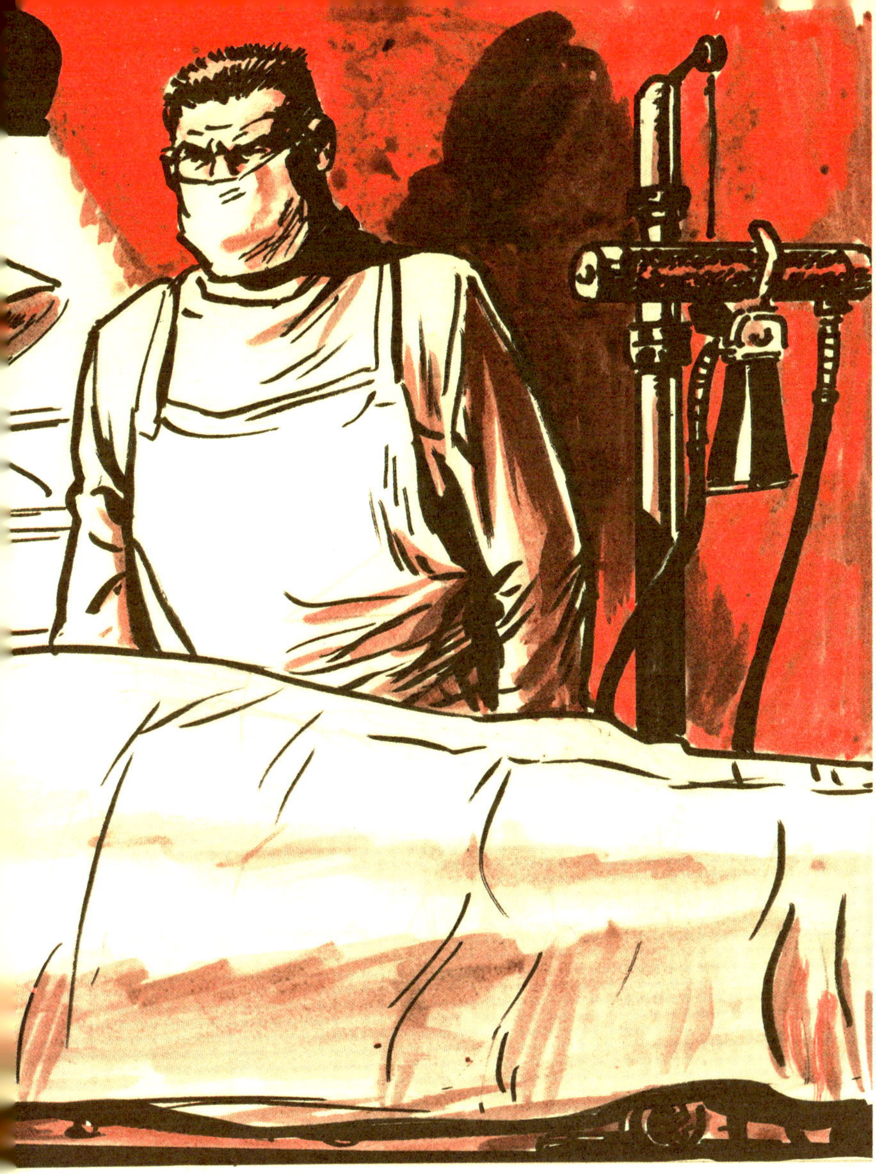

robots; destroying two space shuttles and finally clashing with Sintek, the bionic man.

Sintek had been the creation of the late Professor Sintek — a scientific genius — who had taken the body of a motorcycle crash victim and turned it into a marvel of micro-electronic engineering, complete with nuclear heart and bionic limbs, all controlled by an amazing computer brain.

Adopting the name of his creator, Sintek had vowed to bring Gunter's brother Anton to justice. But both had been destroyed in an explosion.

Gunter had discovered the books containing details of Sintek's creation, which had been stolen by Anton and placed in a safe-deposit box.

Now he planned to use them for his own ends!

His thoughts were interrupted by the arrival of his assistant.

"All is ready, Herr Doctor," the man announced.

"Good!" exclaimed Weltmann. "Then let us begin, Max!"

He picked up the head and followed his assistant down a flight of stairs and into a basement that had been converted into an operating theatre.

The body of the luckless Barney Coleman lay on a surgical table covered by a sheet, with a life-support machine emitting its monotonous bleep.

"Scalpel!" snapped Weltmann, having put on a white gown and gauze mask. He studied the open books of Sintek's creation, then with nerveless hands, made the first incision.

For the next three hours, the two men toiled under the brilliant overhead lights, pausing only to wipe the sweat from their foreheads.

At last, Weltmann straightened up and ripped the mask from his face.

"It is done," he gasped. "Sintek lives again! Monitor his breathing and give him a two hundred and fifty milligram injection every hour. I am going to get some sleep!"

"Yes, Herr Doctor," replied Max subserviently, wondering to himself when *he* was going to get some rest.

Gunter Weltmann was awakened by loud screams. He ran down the stairs into the basement and flung open the operating theatre door.

A muscular figure clad only in shorts had Max by the throat!

Weltmann grabbed a small control pad from a side table and jabbed at a button. The half-naked figure suddenly became motionless, looking like some magnificent Greek statue!

Max disentangled himself from the grasping hands and slumped in a chair.

"He awoke, master . . . and . . . attacked me!" he gasped, fighting for breath.

"Of course he would," replied Weltmann derisively. "He's not conditioned yet!"

He stared at the marble-like face.

"Listen to me, Sintek . . . I am your master. I have equipped you with a new body . . . given you new life! When I press this button again, you will obey everything I say, without question."

His finger hovered over the control pad, then pressed firmly.

The figure rose to its full height and stood staring at him blankly.

"I am yours to command, O Master," he said stiffly.

"We've done it! We've done it!" shouted Max, prancing around in maniacal delight.

"Not yet we haven't — not by a long way!" Weltmann answered thoughtfully. "We've got the body, but not the face. Now listen, Sintek . . . this is what I want you to do . . ."

KIDNAP!

COMMANDER Virgil Grant was looking forward to a round of golf. It had been a long and tedious week with the training of the new recruits, and he felt the need for relaxation.

As he dumped his clubs in the back of the smart convertible standing in the drive of his house, he didn't give a second glance to the black saloon parked in the road outside.

Grant swung the car out into the lane and gunned the engine. The big V8 responded to the accelerator with a throaty growl. He smiled to himself as the wind whipped up his hair. It made a change to have some speed, after all, the crate he was used to driving could only do thirty miles an hour flat out!

He checked his rear-view mirror. A car was right on his tail!

"You're too close for comfort, pal!" he thought to himself. "So I've got to lose you!"

The turbo-charger came into action with a roar, as Grant pressed the gas pedal to the floor. The rev-counter needle swung round the dial and the speedometer quickly reached the 120 mph mark.

But still the black saloon kept pace. Then, suddenly, it pulled out and drew alongside, forcing the sports car towards the verge.

Grant glanced sideways at the driver, who sat impassively behind dark glasses, staring straight ahead.

"What's your game, pal?" Grant yelled above the engine and wind noise. "Stop cutting me up!"

The front wings of the vehicles came into contact, and the impact sent Grant's car ploughing into dense undergrowth!

Next moment, there was a metallic 'clang' as the front wings of the vehicles came into contact. The impact wrenched the steering wheel to the right in Grant's hands. He fought to control it, but the car mounted the verge and ploughed into the dense undergrowth lining the road.

Shaken, but otherwise unhurt, Grant jumped out and ran towards the black saloon, which had halted some twenty metres farther on.

"You stupid maniac!" he yelled. "I ought to — !"

He stopped in his tracks and stared at the small dart that had suddenly appeared in his left arm. A numb feeling came over him, then blackness.

The saloon car driver tucked the dart gun into his black leather jacket and pulled some bushes around the convertible. Then he mechanically walked to the motionless body, picked it up and carefully placed it in the saloon's boot.

"You have done well, Sintek!" said Gunter Weltmann appraisingly, as he examined the unconscious form of Virgil Grant lying on the operating table. He turned to his assistant.

"Come, Max, it is time we put your plastic surgery skill to the test!"

Sintek was placed side by side with Grant on the table.

"Remember, Max . . . it must be perfect!" insisted Weltmann, as the man examined the two faces, picking up a surgical knife.

"Wonderful! Wonderful!" Weltmann exclaimed an hour later.

"Working with Sintek's plastic skin is much better than normal human tissue," replied Max proudly. "And having the real thing as a model, made all the difference. You'd never tell them apart now!"

Minutes later, Grant recovered consciousness.

"What . . . where am I?" he muttered dazedly.

"You're in safe hands, Commander Grant. All we want to know is your secret code sign," answered Weltmann.

"I don't know what you're talking about!" Grant retorted. "Who are you and why have you kidnapped me? I —". His voice tailed away as he caught sight of the man standing next to him. He could have been looking in a mirror . . . for it was an exact copy of himself!

"I had hoped that you wouldn't make this difficult," sighed Weltmann. "But no matter . . . Sintek, find out what we want to know!"

The re-created man took hold of Grant's arms in a grip of iron and stared into his face. Strange beams came from Sintek's eyes.

"The secret code," repeated Sintek.

"Four, one, three . . . alpha five . . . delta six . . . eight, nine, zero," answered Grant in a monotone.

"Excellent!" interjected Weltmann. "Now just transcribe Grant's voice pattern into your memory banks, Sintek, and we're ready!"

"It is done, master," replied Sintek a minute later, in a perfect reproduction of Virgil Grant's voice!

"What are you going to do with me?" asked Grant, finding it difficult to believe what was happening.

"I'm afraid we will have to detain you for a couple of days," Weltmann answered, unlocking a door in a corner of the room. "You will find food and drink enough to last you in here."

He propelled Grant forward into a smaller room.

"It's sound-proofed and the door has a time-lock . . . so any escape-attempt is futile."

"What about me, Herr Doctor?" asked Max, as the door slammed shut. "You promised me ten thousand dollars for my work."

"Of course, Max," replied Weltmann opening a drawer. "And here's something I didn't promise you!"

A pistol fitted with a silencer appeared in Weltmann's hand. There was a dull 'phut' as the weapon spoke its deadly message.

"No, no . . . urggh!" gasped Max as he slumped to the floor.

"Dispose of him and then let's get going, Sintek — or should I say 'Commander Grant'!" Weltmann laughed fiendishly.

HIJACK!

It was Sunday, and the top secret naval base on America's west coast was quieter than usual.

Wearing a Commander's uniform and at the wheel of Virgil Grant's car, which he had earlier recovered from its hiding place, Sintek drove up to the security check-point.

An armed guard saluted him.

"Good morning, Commander. Didn't know you were on duty today, sir," came the greeting.

"We've got to go and join some secret NATO exercise . . . just had a cable. It's a darn nuisance . . . messed up my golf!" replied Sintek steadily.

The barrier was raised and he drove through. So far, so good! Fifty metres farther on, he halted the car at another check-point.

"Code, please, sir," asked the sentry at the glass booth.

"Four, one, three . . . alpha five . . . delta six . . . eight, nine, zero," Sintek answered automatically.

The man operated a computer keyboard.

"Okay, Commander . . . you're cleared. Carry on through . . . and have a nice day!"

After parking the car in the space marked with the licence-plate number, Sintek entered a modern operations room.

A naval rating greeted him.

"Voice print check and code, please sir."

Sintek repeated the number and the man consulted a recording machine, before handing him a folder.

"Your sailing orders, sir. She's in berth twenty-seven."

"Thank you," replied Sintek. Weltmann had done a good job of 'hacking' into the naval base computer to plant the fake orders. Sintek left the building and made his way towards the berthing area.

The bulbous, black shape of the nuclear submarine looked forbidding in its concrete bay. A seaman by the gangway snapped to attention as Sintek approached.

"Are all the crew aboard?" Sintek asked curtly.

"Yes, sir, we're all ready to go," came the reply.

As he entered the craft, Sintek's electronic eyes and computer brain began scanning the equipment. It was complicated to say the least, but he surmised that he could handle it on his own. He summoned the captain.

"We're leaving port in fifteen minutes, skipper . . . is everything okay?"

"Yes, Commander . . . we're carrying a full complement of missiles as instructed," answered the officer. "Though it beats me why we're all armed-up . . . it's not a war situation, is it?"

"It's not your job, or mine, to question orders, Captain Edwards!" replied Sintek sharply.

As he set about busying himself with the sailing procedure, the captain had a quiet word with his First Officer.

"Old Grant seems very odd today, Number One," he said thoughtfully. "There's something strange about him that I can't quite figure! For instance, he always calls me 'Eddie', never 'Skipper'."

"Perhaps he's peeved at missing his golf!" said the First Officer with a grin. His voice sounded over the loudspeaker system. "To your stations, men . . . prepare to sail."

Silently, the submarine nosed out into the harbour-channel towards the open sea. When it passed the last breakwater, Sintek gave orders to the helmsman.

"Steer one — two — zero . . . speed twelve knots . . . we'll remain on the surface."

"One-two-zero? But that's *north*!" muttered the helmsman. Then he caught sight of the captain's warning glance and fell silent.

Sintek scanned the controls with his electronic eyes. They alighted on a red button. "Good," he thought to himself, "I've found it!"

After they had been underway for an hour, he pressed the button. An electronic bleeper sounded and lights began flashing. The crew moved quickly to their lockers and began putting on life-jackets.

"Bit early for an 'abandon ship drill' isn't it?" grumbled one.

"It's probably just to keep us on our toes," replied another.

They filed up the hatches in an orderly manner to the deck, where large life-rafts were automatically being ejected and inflating around the vessel.

"All crew are clear of the ship, Commander," announced the captain five minutes later.

"Well, go and join them, Mister Edwards," said Sintek evenly.

As the hatch closed behind the captain, Sintek walked quickly to the main control panel. He typed out a sequence on the touch pads.

Outside, the crew peered through the flaps of the canopied life rafts.

"Hope he doesn't keep us out here long. It's a bit chilly," moaned a seaman.

Then, the First Officer gave a gasp.

"Look, skipper . . . the securing ropes of the rafts have been cast off!"

The captain watched grimly as the submarine moved slowly away.

"This may sound crazy, Number One . . . but I think our sub has been hijacked!"

From the conning tower of the submarine, Sintek used his telescopic vision to scan the ocean ahead. Soon, he picked out the white turbulence left by a bow-wave. Minutes later, a power boat came into view. The driver cut the engine as he came alongside.

"No problems, Sintek?" queried Gunter Weltmann, stepping on to the sub's deck.

"Everything has gone according to plan, master," Sintek replied.

"Good! Let us go below and send our radio message," said Weltmann triumphantly.

He settled himself in the seat in front of the transmitting equipment.

"This is U.S. Submarine Adventurer calling the Pentagon . . . do you read me?"

There was a pause, then the radio crackled into life.

"Affirmative, Adventurer. But there has been a computer irregularity . . . your orders are to return to port!"

Weltmann laughed fiendishly.

"We're returning to port all right — in Sakhalin!"

The controller at the Pentagon nearly swallowed his microphone.

"But that's a Soviet base!" he exclaimed.

"That's right," replied Weltmann. "They are paying me twenty million dollars for this submarine and its weapons! I have a bionic man with me, called Sintek, whose computer brain has complete mastery over the nuclear missile system we are carrying. If you attempt to stop us, we will wipe out ten major American cities — including Washington! As a warning, a missile without a nuclear warhead will be fired at Disneyland in one hour."

As the transmission ceased, the controller took off his headset.

"Inform the President," he said quietly.

SUMMONED!

SPORTS promoter Hal Ford looked at the bedside clock. It showed five a.m. "Who the heck was thumping on his door at this hour of the morning?" he wondered as he got out of bed, reaching for a dressing gown.

"Hal Ford?" inquired one of the three burly men in raincoats standing outside the door.

"That's what it says on my bell, buddy!" replied Hal, irritably.

"CIA . . . come with us, please.

We've got a car waiting," said one, flipping open a card in a leather case.

The men grabbed him by the arms and propelled him towards the elevator.

"Hey, what's all this about? Can't I get dressed, first?" Hal protested.

"We'll fix you up with a suit, before you meet the President, " grunted one of the men as they got into the car.

"Not THE President?" gasped Hal.

"You got it in one, pal!" came the laconic reply. "He flew into L.A. an hour ago."

The CIA building in Los Angeles was in a turmoil! Armed guards patrolled every floor and staff rushed back and forth along corridors carrying files and armfuls of paper work.

Dressed in a smart grey suit, Hal was ushered into an outer office, where a familiar figure was waiting.

"Brad . . . Brad Dillman!" Hal exclaimed. "What's this all about?"

The middle-aged agent rose from his desk wearily.

"Hi, Hal . . . remember Sintek?"

"How could I ever forget him," replied Hal. "That guy was the finest sportsman the world has ever known. The years I spent with him, were the most exciting of my life . . . until that nutter Anton got himself and Sintek killed!"

Brad took a deep breath.

"I've got news for you, Hal. Anton had a brother named Gunter, who has re-created Sintek and used him to hijack one of our nuclear subs!"

"Whaaaat?" exclaimed Hal. "Sintek's alive?"

Brad led him into an impressive inner office. The President and two of his aides were watching a TV monitor screen.

"What are they looking at a picture of Disneyland for?" thought Hal.

"Two minutes to go, Mister President," said one of the men. "Then we'll find out if Weltmann is bluffing or not!"

Suddenly, there was a big explosion in the picture on the screen and the magnificent Disneyland fairy castle disintegrated into a pile of rubble.

"I guess he means business," said the President grimly. "It's just as well we took the precaution of evacuating the area."

Brad Dillman stepped forward.

"Excuse me, Mister President, but this is Hal Ford."

Grey, steely eyes regarded Hal for a moment. Then the President spoke.

"Mister Ford, we have the greatest National emergency ever on our hands. I understand that you were friendly with this Sintek?"

"Y-yes, sir . . . we were buddies for a long time," stuttered Hal.

"Then you appear to be our only hope of reasoning with him. Do your best . . . America — and the world — are counting on you! I am not exaggerating when I say that your life could be in grave danger if you take on this mission!"

"I'm used to taking risks, Mister President — I'll do whatever you want," said Hal, not feeling the slightest bit as brave as he sounded!

A huge explosion turned Disneyland's fairy castle into a pile of rubble!

SHOW-DOWN!

THREE hours later, a helicopter touched down on the landing pad aboard an American warship. An admiral was waiting to greet the passengers.

"Welcome aboard, Mister Ford . . . Mister Dillman. We'll be overhauling the sub in about twenty minutes."

Hal and Dillman watched the frigate's bow cutting through the water.

"What if Sintek doesn't remember me — he's been completely re-built remember," said Hal.

"We'll worry about that when it happens," replied Brad. Then he pointed ahead. "Look! There she is . . .".

The warship closed on the submarine and then slowed on to a parallel course. Sintek and Weltmann appeared in the conning tower.

"The fools!" screamed Weltmann. "They're going to try to stop us. Use the torpedoes to sink them, Sintek!"

"No, wait," the bionic man replied. His telescopic eyes alighted on the figure at the rail of the warship. Something stirred in his memory banks . . . the man looked familiar.

The figure spoke through a loud hailer.

"Sintek, it's Hal . . . Hal Ford. Remember all the good times we used to have together?"

"Hal . . .?" The re-created man's computer brain ran through millions of entries in its data-base.

"Remember how you fought to save America from that maniac Anton?" Hal went on. "Well, now you're helping to betray your country, by delivering one of its most important defence secrets to the enemy!"

An officer came up to the Admiral beside Hal.

"Two Soviet warships are reported heading this way, sir," he said.

"We'll be out of territorial waters soon . . . then there'll be nothing we can do!" the Admiral replied grimly.

Hal operated the hailer again.

"Sintek, you mustn't help that man with you — he's Anton Weltmann's brother! He'll kill you when you've delivered the sub!"

"That's enough!" yelled Weltmann. "Get below, Sintek!"

"Yes, O Master," replied the bionic man meekly.

The hatch closed and the submarine began to dive.

"Well, that's it," said the Admiral resignedly. "The sub will be in enemy hands in less than an hour! You did your best, Mister Ford."

They watched as the ripples of the diving submarine disappeared.

Suddenly, there was a tremendous explosion and water spout from the spot, followed by more explosions. Then the shattered bow of the submarine broke the surface, before plunging back into the depths.

"Glory be!" exclaimed the Admiral. "He must have detonated the torpedoes in their tubes!"

"You did it, Hal!" yelled Brad Dillman. "Sintek must have remembered you after all!"

Hal watched the widening oil-slick for a moment.

"Yeah, well do me a favour, Admiral," he said in a choked voice. "When your divers go down to recover the missiles, don't let them bring up what's left of my buddy, to stick in a glass case again!"

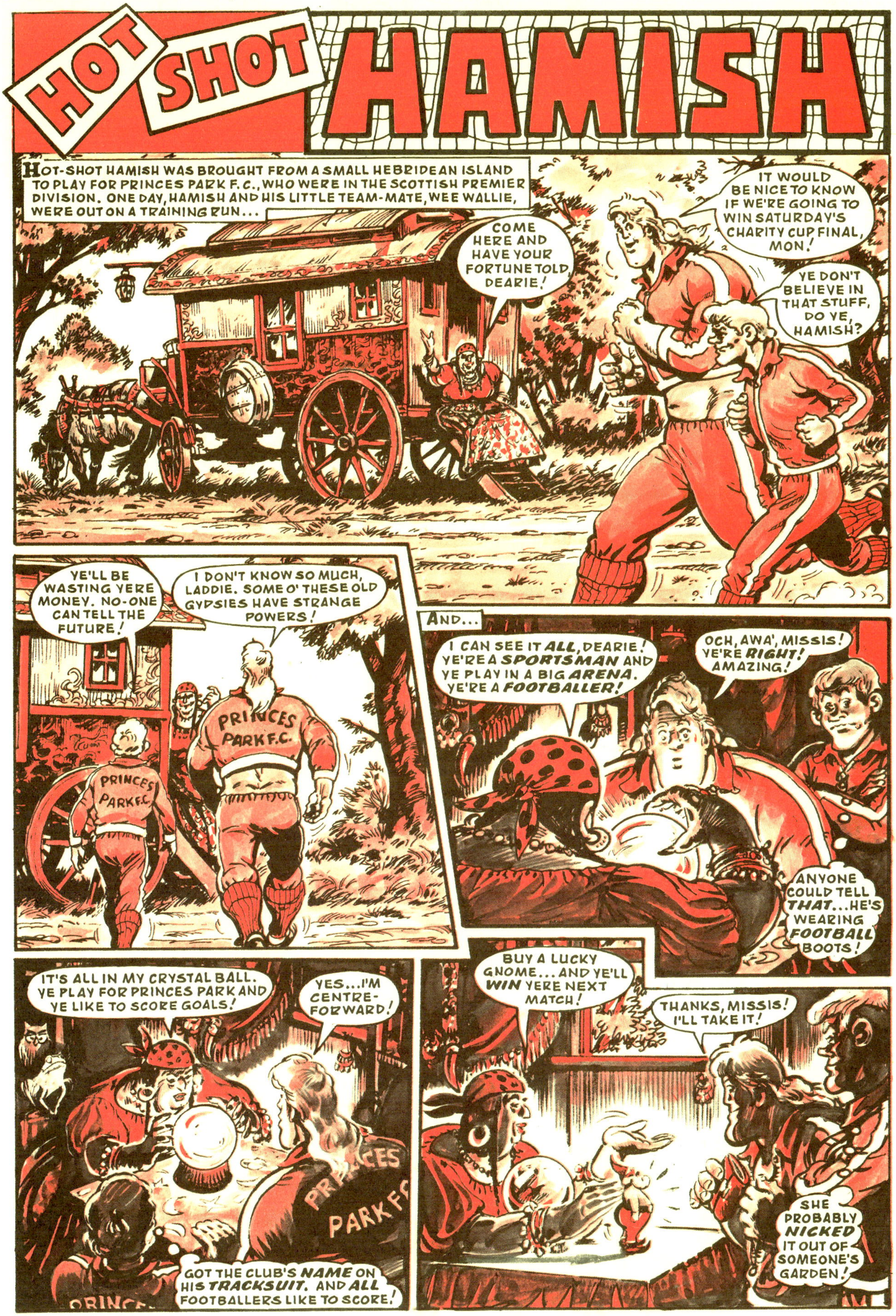
HOT SHOT HAMISH
HOT-SHOT HAMISH WAS BROUGHT FROM A SMALL HEBRIDEAN ISLAND TO PLAY FOR PRINCES PARK F.C., WHO WERE IN THE SCOTTISH PREMIER DIVISION. ONE DAY, HAMISH AND HIS LITTLE TEAM-MATE, WEE WALLIE, WERE OUT ON A TRAINING RUN...
COME HERE AND HAVE YOUR FORTUNE TOLD, DEARIE!
IT WOULD BE NICE TO KNOW IF WE'RE GOING TO WIN SATURDAY'S CHARITY CUP FINAL, MON!
YE DON'T BELIEVE IN THAT STUFF, DO YE, HAMISH?
YE'LL BE WASTING YERE MONEY. NO-ONE CAN TELL THE FUTURE!
I DON'T KNOW SO MUCH, LADDIE. SOME O' THESE OLD GYPSIES HAVE STRANGE POWERS!
PRINCES PARK F.C.
PRINCES PARK F.C.
AND...
I CAN SEE IT ALL, DEARIE! YE'RE A SPORTSMAN AND YE PLAY IN A BIG ARENA. YE'RE A FOOTBALLER!
OCH, AWA', MISSIS! YE'RE RIGHT! AMAZING!
ANYONE COULD TELL THAT...HE'S WEARING FOOTBALL BOOTS!
IT'S ALL IN MY CRYSTAL BALL. YE PLAY FOR PRINCES PARK AND YE LIKE TO SCORE GOALS!
YES...I'M CENTRE-FORWARD!
PRINCES PARK F
GOT THE CLUB'S NAME ON HIS TRACKSUIT. AND ALL FOOTBALLERS LIKE TO SCORE!
BUY A LUCKY GNOME... AND YE'LL WIN YERE NEXT MATCH!
THANKS, MISSIS! I'LL TAKE IT!
SHE PROBABLY NICKED IT OUT OF SOMEONE'S GARDEN!

NOT BAD FOR FIVE POUNDS, EH? IT'S A LUCKY GNOME. I'D BETTER TAKE CARE OF IT, OR WE WON'T WIN ON SATURDAY!
YE'RE DAFT IF YE BELIEVE THAT RUBBISH. YE'VE MORE MONEY THAN SENSE!
FRIDAY... PRINCES PARK TRAINED...
WHAT'S THAT HORRIBLE-LOOKING OBJECT?
HAMISH'S LUCKY GNOME. HE THINKS WE WON'T WIN THE CUP ON SATURDAY IF THE GNOME ISN'T THERE!
NO SUCH THING AS LUCK IN FOOTBALL! IT'S ALL HARD WORK... AND SKILL. I DON'T WANT GNOMES HANGING ABOUT HERE!
OCH, YE SHOULDNA HAVE DONE THAT, MISTER MCWHACKER. I'M GETTING IT BACK!
MOTORS
DRINK
THE ORNAMENT LANDED ON THE ROOF OF A PASSING VEHICLE.
YE'VE HAD IT, HAMISH. THE LORRY'S ON THE MOVE.
I'M NO' LETTING MY GNOME GO. I'M GOING AFTER IT, MON!
WHAT'S THAT GREAT HIGHLAND HAGGIS-EATING TWIT DOING?
GETTING HIS GNOME BACK. HE DOESN'T WANT TO BE GNOME-LESS! HAW, HAW! GET IT, BOSS? GNOME-LESS! HOMELESS!
OCH, THEY DINNA BUILD THINGS AS STRONG AS THEY USED TO!

OOOOERR! THERE- THERE'S SOMETHING IN HERE!
SINGSTER'S CIRCUS
OCH, THE GNOME IS LUCKY! THE LION'S ASLEEP. I HOPE HE STAYS THAT WAY!
SCHIAFFINO!
SOME TIME LATER...
HELLO, MISTER. I-I'M JUST GETTING MY GNOME BACK!
AYE! AND YE'VE BUSTED THE TOP O' MY LION-CAGE. YE'LL HAVE TO PAY FOR THAT, MY LAD!
I HAVEN'T ANY MONEY ON ME, MISTER! SORRY!
ALL RIGHT... YOU CAN WORK FOR WHAT YE OWE! I'LL GIVE YE A GOOD JOB. THE BIGGEST JOB IN THE CIRCUS!
YE CAN SCRUB MY ELEPHANT... THAT'S THE BIGGEST JOB IN THE CIRCUS! HAW, HAW!
OKAY, IF YE SAY SO, SIR!
I'LL HAVE TO GO AS SOON AS I'VE FINISHED! I'M DUE BACK AT PRINCES PARK FOR THE CUP MATCH TOMORROW! THEY'LL BE WORRIED ABOUT ME!
YE CAN CALL THE CLUB AND TELL THEM WHERE YE ARE, IF YE LIKE. IT'LL BE A TRUNK CALL! HAW, HAW... GET IT?

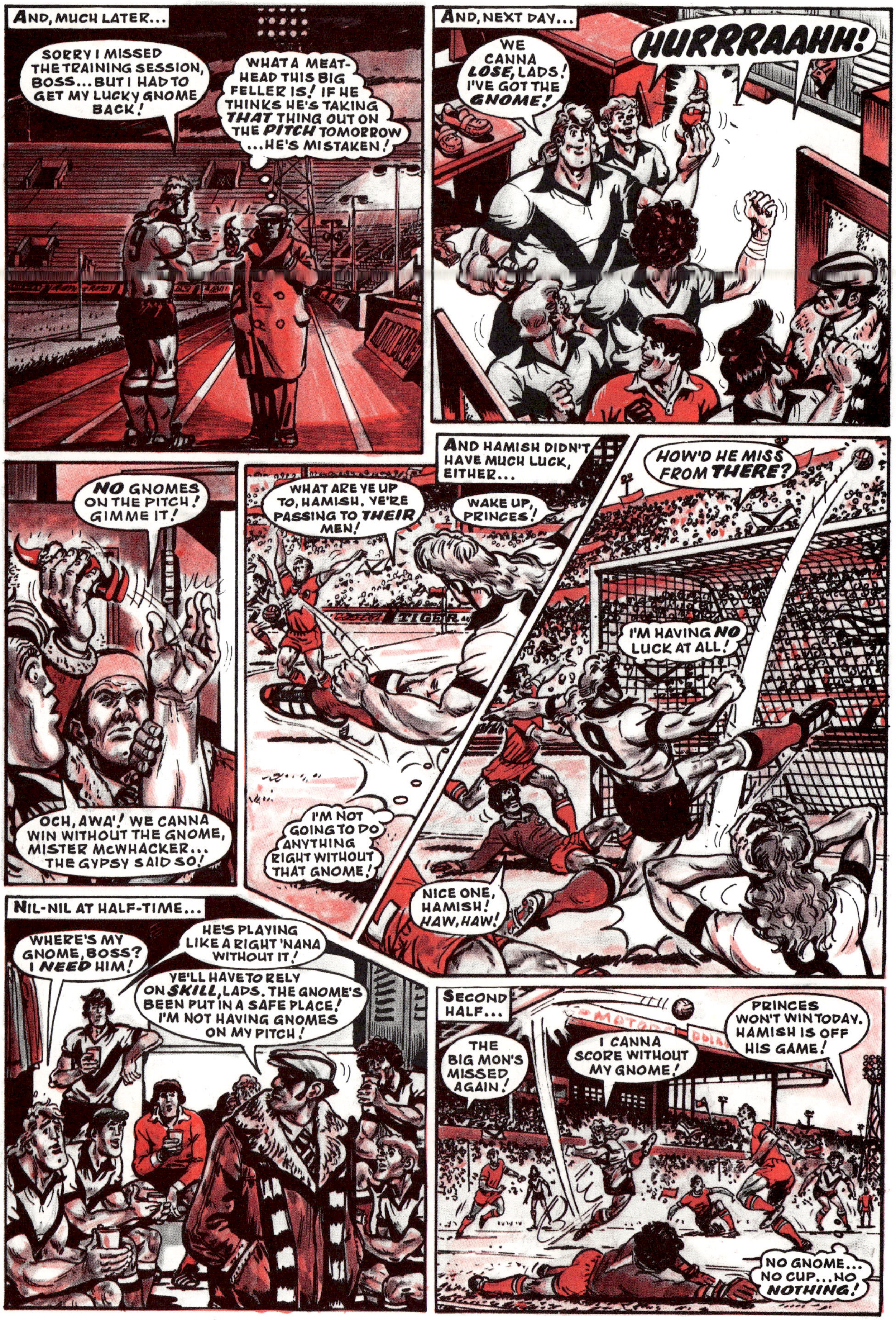
AND, MUCH LATER...
SORRY I MISSED THE TRAINING SESSION, BOSS... BUT I HAD TO GET MY LUCKY GNOME BACK!
WHAT A MEAT-HEAD THIS BIG FELLER IS! IF HE THINKS HE'S TAKING THAT THING OUT ON THE PITCH TOMORROW ...HE'S MISTAKEN!
AND, NEXT DAY...
HURRRAAHH!
WE CANNA LOSE, LADS! I'VE GOT THE GNOME!
NO GNOMES ON THE PITCH! GIMME IT!
OCH, AWA'! WE CANNA WIN WITHOUT THE GNOME, MISTER McWHACKER... THE GYPSY SAID SO!
AND HAMISH DIDN'T HAVE MUCH LUCK, EITHER...
WHAT ARE YE UP TO, HAMISH. YE'RE PASSING TO THEIR MEN!
WAKE UP, PRINCES!
TIGER
I'M NOT GOING TO DO ANYTHING RIGHT WITHOUT THAT GNOME!
HOW'D HE MISS FROM THERE?
I'M HAVING NO LUCK AT ALL!
NICE ONE, HAMISH! HAW, HAW!
NIL-NIL AT HALF-TIME...
WHERE'S MY GNOME, BOSS? I NEED HIM!
HE'S PLAYING LIKE A RIGHT 'NANA WITHOUT IT!
YE'LL HAVE TO RELY ON SKILL, LADS. THE GNOME'S BEEN PUT IN A SAFE PLACE! I'M NOT HAVING GNOMES ON MY PITCH!
SECOND HALF...
THE BIG MON'S MISSED AGAIN!
I CANNA SCORE WITHOUT MY GNOME!
PRINCES WON'T WIN TODAY. HAMISH IS OFF HIS GAME!
NO GNOME... NO CUP... NO NOTHING!

THE MINUTES TICKED AWAY... AND STILL NO SCORE...
IT'S YERE LAST CHANCE O' WINNING, PRINCES! GET IT IN THE NET!
THERE'S NO USE PASSING TO HAMISH... HE'S HOPELESS!
I'LL GO IT ALONE! ALL THE WAY!
THEN...
PENALTY!
BOOOOOO!
SHAME! WEE WALLIE WAS RIGHT THROUGH!
TAKE IT, HAMISH!
GIVE IT THE HOT-SHOT, MON!
YE SCORE... AND WE'VE WON!
I CANNA DO IT, LADS. I'D MISS. I MUST HAVE MY GNOME TO BRING ME LUCK!
MISTER McWHACKER WAS FURIOUS!
THE BIG MON'S GONE TO PIECES! HE'S ALL OF A JELLY! I'D BETTER GET THE ROTTEN LITTLE GNOME... OR HE'LL NEVER KNOCK THAT PENALTY IN!
AND...
TAKE THE PENALTY, HAMISH! HERE'S YERE STUPID GNOME!
IT'LL BE ALL RIGHT, HAMISH!
I CANNA MISS, NOW!
IF YE DINNA TAKE THE PENALTY SOON... I'LL SEND YE ALL OFF!

THEN...
IT'S THERE!
THE HOT-SHOT PENALTY!
HAMISH SCORES!
NOW YE CAN GO BACK IN THE DUSTBIN! HAMISH SCORED BECAUSE HE PRACTISES PENALTY-KICKS EVERY DAY! IT'S NOT LUCK!
WE WON THE CUP FOR YE, BOSS!
LAST-MINUTE PENALTY! DRAMATIC, EH?
GOOD JOB YE FOUND THAT GNOME!
WHERE'S HAMISH?
HE'LL BE HERE IN A MOMENT, BOSS... HE'S GONE TO GET SOMETHING!
THEN...
THE GYPSY LADY LET ME HAVE THEM!
WE'VE GOT TO BE THE LUCKIEST TEAM IN SCOTLAND NOW, LADS!
WE'LL SCORE HUNDREDS OF GOALS!
NEVER LOSE!
ONE FOR EVERY MON IN THE TEAM! THEY'RE ALL BARMY!

GRAND SLAM FOR SCOTLAND!

ROAD TO THE GRAND SLAM

WALES	9	SCOTLAND	15
SCOTLAND	18	ENGLAND	6
IRELAND	9	SCOTLAND	32
SCOTLAND	21	FRANCE	12

Scotland began their 1984 Rugby Union Championship campaign with a tough away game at Cardiff Arms Park. Here the Scots half back John Rutherford bursts past Wales' Mark Titley.

V WALES

Scottish captain Jim Aitken is congratulated by team-mates John Rutherford and David Leslie, after scoring his first international try, and the match-winner against Wales.

THE SCOTS TRIUMPH OVER ENGLAND, IRELAND, WALES AND FRANCE FOR THE FIRST TIME IN 59 YEARS!

V ENGLAND

The next obstacle on Scotland's glory path was the 100th Calcutta Cup match against England. And despite the fact that the Auld Enemy held a 47 victories to 36 advantage, the Scots showed no mercy, with a triumphant Alexander Kennedy, above, scoring their second try under the posts, with the Murrayfield scoreboard recording a great win, above right. Now only Ireland stood between Scotland and their first Triple Crown for 46 years. Despite spectacular passing from Ireland's Tony Doyle, right, the Scots led 22-0 with just over half an hour gone! Keith Robertson (13, below) added to Scotland's total in the 2nd half with this fine try.

V IRELAND

GRAND SLAM FOR SCOTLAND!

V FRANCE

The Triple Crown won, Scotland came to their final match against France. Both sides were unbeaten, and things looked grim for Scotland when they were 3-9 down after an hour. But the courageous Scots rallied and levelled at 12-12 with eleven minutes left, then scored twice more, including their only try, by Jim Calder, top above. After the match, Scotland skipper Jim Aitken, above, could hardly believe he'd led his side into the history books!

AN EXCITING SKID SOLO STORY THAT FIRST APPEARED IN A 1967 ISSUE OF TIGER!

NOT EVEN THE FAMOUS RACE ACE COULD CONTROL THE CAR ON THE ICY SURFACE!

IT WAS A GOOD JOB THERE WAS NO SPEEDO ON THE HURTLING 'SLED'!

Autograph ALBERT
I'M GOING TO WATCH THE WEIGH-IN FOR TONIGHT'S BIG FIGHT!
BIG FIGHT
LEFTY SMITH VS. RIGHT HOOK HOOLEY
HERE THEY COME!
THIS IS EXCITING!
HURRAY!
GRUNT!
GRUNT! GRUNT!
HEY, STOP PUSHING!
OKAY, LEFTY, GET ON THE SCALES!
OOPS! I'M ALSO ON THE SCALES—AND THERE'S NO ROOM TO GET OFF!
THEN...
YOU'RE SIX STONE OVERWEIGHT! YOU'LL HAVE TO GET THAT REDUCED BY TONIGHT!
GULP!
SHAME!
AND SO, FOR THE NEXT HOUR!
PERHAPS I SHOULD TELL HIM WHAT HAPPENED?
SKIP!
AND THEN ANOTHER HOUR...
IT'S TOO HORRIBLE EVEN TO WATCH!
FASTER!
SAG!
SAGGER!
EVENTUALLY...
GOOD GRIEF! YOU'RE TWENTY POUNDS UNDER YOUR FIGHTING WEIGHT!
SWOON!
I'M NOT TOUCHING 'EM THIS TIME!
QUICK—GET ALL THE CREAM BUNS, CAKES AND GOODIES YOU CAN LAY YOUR HANDS ON!
I'LL GIVE THEM A HAND!
DRESSING ROOM.
LATER...
IS HE READY?
NO—WE'RE GIVING UP THE FIGHT GAME. I DIDN'T REALISE HE COULD EAT SO MUCH. WE'RE ENTERING FOR BUN EATING CONTESTS INSTEAD!
FULL
AND THAT LITTLE LAD COULD BE A CHAMPION ONE DAY!

The TOUGH GAME

TWENTY MINUTES LATER...
YOU'RE NOT GOING TO EAT ALL THAT LOT, ARE YOU, APE-MAN?
'COURSE I AM... GOT TO KEEP MY STRENGTH UP, OR I'LL END UP A SHRIMP LIKE YOU TWO!
THE DAY OF THE BIG MATCH.
RIGHT, LADS... I WANT A HUNDRED AND TEN PER CENT EFFORT FROM YOU! WIN THIS ONE AND YOU'RE ONLY A MATCH AWAY FROM WEMBLEY!
POTTS
WE WON'T LET YOU DOWN, BOSS... THE BIG THREE ARE HERE!
POTTERDALE BEGAN WELL AGAINST THEIR OPPONENTS, REDWOOD...
WITH YOU, JACKIE!
TAKE IT, MAN...
WE'VE HAD FIVE TACKLES... GIVE IT THE BOOT, ERNIE!
RIGHT, THAT'LL PUT SOME PRESSURE ON'EM...
THE REDWOOD FULL-BACK COMPLETELY MIS-JUDGED THE BOUNCE OF BIG ERNIE'S KICK...
HE THOUGHT IT WAS GOING INTO TOUCH!
THAT'S MINE!
OHHH!
APE-MAN!
HE'S GOING LIKE A TANK!
MORE LIKE A BATTERING-RAM I'D SAY!
BACK HIM UP, LADS!

BUT APE-MAN DIDN'T NEED ANY HELP!
YES! HE'S THERE!
WHAT A TRY!
CURVE-KICK SPECIALIST CHARLIE TOMMS MADE THE DIFFICULT CONVERSION LOOK EASY!
SIX-NIL TO THE POTTS!
WE'RE GONNA WIN THE CUP! WE'RE GONNA WIN THE CUP!
IT WAS STILL SIX-NIL AT HALF-TIME...
I HEAR THERE ARE SOME FRENCH TALENT-SCOUTS IN THE CROWD, LADS... WITH SOME BIG MONEY TO SPEND ON PLAYERS!
THEY MIGHT MAKE AN OFFER FOR YOU, APE-MAN!
NO CHANCE! BESIDES, THEY COULDN'T AFFORD HIS GRUB BILL! HA, HA!
IN THE SECOND HALF...
WOULDN'T WANT ME, EH... I'LL SHOW BIG-MOUTH ERNIE!
THE OPENING WAS MADE FOR DUGGIE...
GREAT PASS, PAL... YOU'VE TAKEN HALF THE REDWOOD TEAM WITH YOU!
YESSSS! RIGHT BETWEEN THE POSTS!
SCORED BY BATSON, BUT MADE BY APE-MAN!
DUGGIE MADE THE EASY CONVERSION, BUT THEN REDWOOD CAME BACK STRONGLY...
GO, GO, GO, YOU REDS!
BRING HIM DOWN, POTTS!
CAN'T...TOO ...TRICKY...

But Ape-Man stood firm!
GOTCHA!
WELL STOPPED!
Full time...
TWELVE-NIL!
POTTS ARE ON THE WAY TO WEMBLEY!
WELL DONE, LADS... I'M RIGHT PROUD OF YOU!
In the dressing room...
THERE'S A COUPLE OF FOREIGN BLOKES TO SEE YOU OUTSIDE, APE-MAN...
ME?
I RECKON IT'S THOSE FRENCH SCOUTS!
It was!
AH, MONSIEUR APE-MAN... FORMIDABLE PLAY! WE WOULD BE PREPARED TO PAY YOU FIVE THOUSAND FRANCS A WEEK TO PLAY FOR ST. GALLION!
YOU MUST COME TO FRANCE TO SEE OUR CLUB, TO 'ELP YOU MAKE UP YOUR MIND!
COR!
Two days later, Ape-Man had a letter...
A FIRST-CLASS AIR TICKET TO PARIS!
YOU'RE NOT REALLY THINKING OF LEAVING POTTERDALE, APE-MAN?
WHO ISN'T! I'VE JUST FOUND OUT THAT FIVE THOUSAND FRANCS IS FIVE HUNDRED QUID A WEEK!
They went to see Mister Wildman...
WELL, GOOD LUCK, LAD... I WOULDN'T STAND IN YOUR WAY, IF YOU CAN BETTER YOURSELF!
THANKS, BOSS...
WE'RE GOING OVER TO FRANCE IN DUGGIE'S CAR TO KEEP AN EYE ON APE-MAN!
And so...
BONJOUR, M'SIEUR APE-MAN — WELCOME TO FRANCE!
WE 'AVE A CAR AT YOUR DISPOSAL...
OH, BONGER TO YOU, TOO, MATE!

ALL ST. GALLION PLAYERS HAVE A CAR—FREE!
WOW!
YOU LIKE TO TRY IT?
ST GALLION
BUT!
GET OUT OF IT, YOU IMBECILE!
AAAAH! YOU ARE DRIVING ON THE WRONG SIDE OF THE ROAD!
CAFE
TABA
SACRE BLEU! YOU 'AVE NO LICENCE?
I'LL BE BETTER WHEN I'VE PASSED MY TEST!
SOMEHOW THEY GOT TO THE ST. GALLION GROUND, WHERE DUGGIE AND ERNIE WERE WAITING...
HI, APE-MAN... THIS IS A POSH PLACE, AIN'T IT?
YEAH, BETTER THAN POTTERDALE!
'E PLAYS RUGBY BETTER THAN HE DRIVES, THANK GOODNESS!
ST GALL
APE-MAN TOOK PART IN A PRACTICE MATCH...
OOOOOF! HE IS TOO STRONG FOR US!
SUCH POWER AND DRIVE... FORMIDABLE!
EASY! DID YOU ENJOY THE RIDE, FELLERS?
WHAT A KICK!
WE MUST HAVE THIS PLAYER... HE WILL BE A GREAT ASSET TO THE TEAM!
FANTASTIC DISPLAY, M'SIEUR! THIS IS OUR PRESIDENT...
WE ARE HOLDING A BANQUET TONIGHT IN YOUR HONOUR, M'SIEUR APE-MAN ...THEN YOU WILL SIGN FOR ST. GALLION, YES?
YEAH, I'M GONNA LIKE IT HERE!

LATER...
YOU CAN'T BE SERIOUS ABOUT JOINING THIS FRENCH CLUB, APE-MAN?
I AM! THEY'VE OFFERED ME A POSH HOUSE, TOO... BETTER THAN MY DUMP BACK HOME!
OH, NO!
ST GALLION BANQUET
ST GALLION WELCOMES APE-MAN
HURRAH!
GOSH! LOOK AT ALL THIS!
THIS WAY, M'SIEUR APE-MAN...
THANKS, PAL... I COULD JUST DO WITH SOME GRUB!
WHAT WOULD M'SIEUR LIKE FOR HORS-D'OEUVRE... SNAILS OR FROGS' LEGS?
URRRGH! NO THANKS! AIN'T YOU GOT NO PIES OR FISH AN' CHIPS?
I AM SORRY, M'SIEUR... PERHAPS YOU WOULD LIKE COQ AU VIN OR DUCK A LA ORANGE?
WHAT'S THAT ... IT LOOKS HORRIBLE!
SORRY, MATE... BUT I WOULDN'T BE ANY GOOD TO YOUR CLUB IF I CAN'T GET DECENT GRUB — THE DEAL'S OFF!
B-BUT...
HURRAH! APE-MAN'S STAYING AT POTTS!
WHEN THEY GOT BACK TO ENGLAND...
THIS IS THE STUFF TO KEEP ME AT POTTERDALE FOR EVER!
WANT SOME FRENCH MUSTARD ON YOUR SAUSAGES, APE-MAN! HA, HA!

Published by IPC Magazines Ltd., King's Reach Tower, Stamford Street, London SE1 9LS. Sole agents for Australia and New Zealand: Gordon & Gotch Ltd., South Africa: Central News Agency. Printed and bound by Casterman S.A. Belgium. SBN 85037 616 5.